A
History
of the Parish of
Marchwiel

Cynthia Rees

bridge
books

Wrexham

First published in Wales in 1998
by
BRIDGE BOOKS
61 Park Avenue
Wrexham
LL12 7AW

In memory of my parents (School House, 1935-72)

A CIP entry for this book is available from the British Library

ISBN 1-872424-73-2

Printed and bound by
MFP, Manchester

Contents

Acknowledgements

I should like to thank all those who have given me the benefit of their time and knowledge in the writing of this book, especually the County Archivists and their helpful staff at the Denbighshire nd Flintshire Record Offices, the staff of the National Library of Wales, the Local Studies Librarian at Wrexham Library, Jeremy Cragg representing the National Trust at Erddig, Eric griffiths for permission to quote from his biography of the first Philip Yorke, and Miss E A (Molly) Preen, who generously allowed me to consult some of her papers and also her copy of notes by the late Mrs Sunter Harrison.

I am also indebted to present and former residents of Marchwiel, who answered with patience my numerous enquiries about their memories of the pre-war village — in particular Councillor J A Davies, Mrs Ena Hamer and Miss Winifred Hunt; to Mr and Mrs Bell of Marchwiel Hall for their hospitality and help; to all the farmers who allowed me to investigate their historic houses and land, to Miss Hamlett, Mrs Doreen Jones, Mrs Susan Miller and all who kindly loaned photographs for inclusion in the book, to the Rector and Churchwardens for allowing access to St Marcella's, and to the Headmaster and staff of Ysgol Deiniol for granting me the space to consult records.

Finally, I pay tribute to the painstaking work done by Mrs Eileen lee and the Clwyd Family History Society in transcribing the parish registers up to the early nineteenth century, making the researcher's task much easier. I should also like to express my sincere gratitude, although more than thirty years have passed since his death, for the encouragement of the late Canon E E Thomas, who made records available to me and passed on his own interest in Marchwiel's history, which he shared with my father.

All royalty profits from the sale of this book will be donated to the Organ Restoration Fund of Marchwiel Church.

Cynthia M Rees
Rhosllanerchrugog
1998

1: The Church from the earliest times

The village of Marchwiel lies about two miles to the south-east of Wrexham on the road to Bangor Isycoed (which is also known as Bangor Monachorum, because of its early connection with Celtic Christianity). In the early Middle Ages, Marchwiel was part of the lordship of Bromfield and Yale, or Welsh Maelor, which played such a prominent role in the history of the Welsh border at that time; its recorded story, however, goes back several centuries before the Norman Conquest and is the starting point of this account.

The close link with the great monastic settlement in Bangor, which probably lay just a mile or so away close to the banks of the Dee, is confirmed by Edward Lluyd in his *Parochialia* (1699); he says that the church in Marchwiel 'was formerly named Daniel's Chappel and they say it belonged to Bangor, as did likewise Worthenbury'. Clearly the connection with St Deiniol (died 584 AD) was commonly known, although the facts about this early period are not easy to establish with certainty; Welsh and Saxon chroniclers, for example, differ in their accounts. The early 7th century was a troubled and barbarous period in the religious and political history of Britain, and in 613 AD the pagan king of Northumbria, Ethelfrith (or -frid), marched South as far as Chester with the intention of driving a wedge between the Welsh of North Wales (or Strathclyde) and their fellow countrymen to the West (modern North Wales). He was met by a Welsh army, supported by members of the Celtic church and possibly including Dunawd, Abbot of Bangor, with several hundred of the brethren, who, it is believed, had established the settlement a few years previously at the instigation of Dunawd's son, Deiniol. As to what happened next, we cannot do better than read the words of Thomas Pennant's *A Tour in Wales*:

> [The King of Powys, leading the Welsh army] ... called to his aid one thousand two hundred religious from the great convent of Bangor and posted them upon a hill in order that he might benefit from their prayers. Ethelfrid fell in with this pious corps, and finding what their business was, put them to the sword without mercy.

Very few of the Welsh — it is said only about fifty — escaped from Chester and we must assume that the Northumbrians followed up their victory by destroying the settlement; at any rate it was probably abandoned soon afterwards and it seems likely that some of the servants of Daniel's Chapel in Marchwiel also suffered. Browne Willis, writing in 1719, says that after the disaster at Chester the parish of

Marchwiel took its name from the materials of which the chapel was built *ie* strong twigs. This is a useful reminder that we must not imagine the foundation at Bangor to have been similar in appearance to Valle Crucis or any of the other familiar ruined abbeys to be seen today, which were not built for another five or six centuries. Indeed the Welsh word Bangor has two meanings - first a monastery or abbey, as in Gwynedd and Northern Ireland as well as locally, but also an enclosure of willow or osiers. Willis's view is accepted by D R Thomas in his *History of the Diocese of St Asaph* and also by Professor Ifor Williams in his book *Enwau Lleoedd* (Place Names). *Gwialen*, plural *gwiail*, has a variety of meanings; in the singular it refers to a rod or stick, and in the plural, osiers or withies or twigs — and the earliest references to the settlement invariably call it Marchwiail.

It is clear that there was a definite link between Deiniol and the first church in Marchwiel, and probably this was maintained throughout the Middle Ages, at least, but strangely there is no written reference in early history to the dedication to St Marcella (Marchell in Welsh); in fact there are at least two saints of that name and the tradition must simply be accepted as it stands. To make the matter even more complicated, some nineteenth century maps refer to the church as dedicated to St Marcellus, another hero of the fifth century church. There appear to be no further direct references to a church building in Marchwiel for many centuries, although there is one belief that Daniel's Chapel was still in existence in the thirteenth century. We are not without proof, however, that worship was continuous; Edward Lluyd's survey in 1699 noted 'their feast on Daniel's tyde' and 'there was a cross near Bryn-y-grog and ye place still called Kroes-y-mab' (the Cross of the son of God); again about the house at Bryn-y-grog, 'here stood an old cross'. The mound which was all that remained of this cross was clearly visible in the field on the right of Marchwiel Hall Lane, opposite Croes-y-mab, when it was described in 1911 by the Royal Commission on Ancient Monuments, as follows:

> In the angle between Bryn-y-grog Hill and the road to Marchwiel Hall, and opposite Croes-y-mab farmhouse, is a small bank having the shape of an irregular letter 'T', the horizontal arm about 20 yards long and the vertical arm about half that length; the whole is raised about 2–3 feet above the general level. Whether this be a comparatively new feature or an old one impaired by time and neglect it is certain that a mediaeval cross (in actual fact probably earlier than mediaeval) once stood near this spot.

The Royal Commission does not mention the second cross, but Edward Lluyd says that the breadth of the parish *o'r Pumrhyd* (Five Fords) on the border with Wrexham to the *Kroesae Gwnnion* (the white or holy crosses) on the border with Bangor is *vilhdir* (one mile). A map compiled in 1715 showed the White Crosses by the side of the road from Marchwiel via Bangor to Whitchurch 'at a point where the Cock Bank crossing now is'. It is possible that Gerwyn Hall — *Gerwyn* meaning near the white or holy — provides another clue, but the best proof we have is one of the Erddig estate maps, dating from about 1715 when John Meller was negotiating to acquire the property. This map provides several field names, including that of Croesau Gwynion, which lies on the right-hand corner at Cock Bank crossroads as we leave Marchwiel. In 1719 the Rector, Dr Ffoulkes, distributed Bibles for the use of the poor, stipulating that they should be passed on to others in due course; one such copy went to Philip Randle of 'Croise Gwynion'. The name occurs again in a note among the Erddig papers dated July 20th 1830 referring to a possible exchange of properties between Simon Yorke II and Sir Watkin Williams Wynn. Perhaps an aerial view of the field would give us more information about its mediaeval history.

After its early connection with Bangor, the next mention of the church in the Middle Ages is found in the Norwich Taxation, carried out by the Bishop of Norwich in 1254 for the purpose of raising revenue for the Crown, as *Ecc'a de Marchocil* in the deanery of Maelor, and again in the Lincoln Taxation of 1291 there is a reference — *Ecclia de Marthwyel Taxat £5 10s.* Much later, in the Valor of 1535 the Rectory is stated to be of the gross value of £13 3s 4d, nett £12 13 4d, tenths to the king £1 5s 4d.

We can be fairly certain therefore that from at least the thirteenth century there was a church on the site of the present building, and that it was used until the late eighteenth century, when it was rebuilt by the parishioners, as one of the windows in the nave confirms:

> *Hasce aedes vetustate dilapidatas restituebant parochiani an'o salutis MDCCLXXVIII.* (The parishioners restored this building in the year of grace 1778 when it was decayed through age.)

Tyddyn Daniel

We are told that in 1562 a smallholding by this name stood on the glebeland in the township of Bedwell, and whether or not it commemorates Daniel — or Deiniol — it enjoys the distinction of being one of the few examples, apart from the church, of continuous occupation of its site for at least four centuries. The property was acquired from the Crown by the church at the end of the reign of James I, and it was to be a frequent financial lifeline when the old building was in constant need of timber and revenue to carry out repairs; the arrangement was confirmed by an Indenture dated 7th January 1628 (4 Charles I) drawn up between, on the one side, Sir Edward Broughton Bt., Owen Brereton of Borras Esq, Robert Sontley of Sontley Esq, Kenrick Edisbury of Bedwell Gent., and John Kenrick of Marchwiel Gent., and on the other side James ap Edward of Bedwell, Yeoman and Elizabeth, wife of the said James. The property is referred to as 'formerly in the tenure of John Wynne ap Edward, deceased, and then in the tenure of the said Sir Edward Broughton (and the others mentioned) at a yearly rent of 20s and 10d, together with all the barns, buildings, pastures, woods etc. Their possession of it (1626) confirmed; they are to have charge of it on behalf of the parish. ... And that the rents, issues and profits might be continued and for ever remain (as the same hath been and continued time out of mind of man) to and for the only use, maintenance and repair of the parish church of Marthwiell and to none other use, intent or purpose whatsoever.'

James ap Edward and his wife were to be the tenants for 21 years, answerable to Sir Edward and the other gentlemen, and to keep the property in good repair. It consisted of some 14 acres and there was also an adjoining tenement of about 12 acres, which was acquired at about the same time for the support of poor persons not receiving parish relief.

The most significant document detailing parish life in the seventeenth and eighteenth centuries is the Vestry Book for the period 1663–1777; indeed it is the only evidence apart from the registers of births, marriages and deaths, and it has been drawn upon extensively to produce this account. There is also a document among the Edisbury/Yorke papers, dated 1656, in which Hugh Lloyd, yeoman, on payment of five shillings, bought a seat from John Edisbury of Pentre Clawdd and his wife Christiana, 'adjoining Westwards on ye steeple of ye said church and eastward on ye pugh of Mrs Margaret Broughton, ye relict of Morgan Broughton late of Marchwiel aforesaid Esq, which said seat did heretofore belong to ye tenement now in the possession of ... of Sontley'. Many such transactions took place in the ensuing centuries, and occupantion rights to one or more pews was often included in the sale particulars of an estate until the 1920s.

From about 1674 onwards there are repeated references to assessments imposed on the villagers for the repair of the church, to be used for the payment of painters, stonemasons and others when the floor was flagged, the roof pointed and the steeple repaired — probably normal wear and tear. A new steeple was built on the old church in 1696, however, causing one writer to remark a few years later that there was a real danger that the new structure was too heavy for the rest of the building. Indeed he describes the church as 'ye scandal of ye neighbourhood'. It was reported to the Bishop in 1749 that 'The Church is small, being but one [a]isle, and in good condition excepting that the Chancel and steeple want some flags, which I have directed to be done by the 1st of August; some of the Seats are irregular and project into the alley ...' The old building contained several memorials which have now disappeared; Owen Brereton, who had signed the Tyddyn Daniel Indenture, and Dorothy his wife, were remembered on 'two flatt stones within ye rails of ye altar partly towards ye North side'.

Brereton was buried on 20th April 1648 and his wife on 4th June 1668. Near them but on the South side lay Robert Ellice Esq 'who exchanged this life for a better, the 9th daye of June 1654'.

We now return to the long list of calls made upon the resources of Tyddyn Daniel:

1722   By order of the vestry it is agreed one of ye present churchwardens should hew as much timber growing upon Tyddyn Daniel as will repair ye roof of ye two bays burnt of ye Rector's house near ye Church

1728   Agreed that the Rector be continued steward to Tyddyn Daniel till ye painting of the East end of the Church be paid for.

1728   Paid for painting and writing the Lord's Prayer, Creed and Ten Commandments —   £10 10s 0d (This painted panel can still be seen in the tower gallery)

1735   Ten trees cut for the repair of the Church from Simon Fenny's tenement

1735   Ordered at vestry that £29 8s 7d raised out of the poor's land in Iscoed be applied to the repair of Marchwiel Church and that ye rents of Tyddyn Daniel beginning at Midsummer last past and thenceforward be appropriated in lieu thereof till the whole be made up. Dec.26th agreed that the old Church plate shall be sold towards the repairs of the Church and that the rent due from Tyddyn Daniel..... be applied towards plastering and finishing the church.

1735   An account of ye repairs done in ye church of Marchwiell Nov. 22nd when ye North and South sides were new made, and a new gallery within.

£29 14s 7d from the poor's money, lent for that use, to be paid back with the rents of Tyddyn Daniel. Also Fenny's Midsummer rent £4. Money from the old plate £4 3s 6d. For old Iron at 1d a pound — 7s. For old timber — 6s. Remainder of the money after slating ye church and paying Timothy Kenrick for cutting down timber and sawing it — £2 12s 9d.

£7 7s 6d spent on brick, £2 on lime; for meat and drink for 22 teams that carried ye brick   £1 11s 0d

to Clubb ye bricklayer   £9 8s 1d
to Powell ye carpenter   £ 8s 6d
to Youd, glazier   £3 5s 7d

1735   Simon Fenny's rent from Tyddyn Daniel laid out in cutting and sawing timber for the church loft.

1735   Paid Dr Ffoulkes when building of ye church being in arrears. Due to him the sum of £0 17s 6d.

1736   Agreed that a cornish be put on the gallery beam and that the Banisters be painted of Mahogany colour out of Tyddyn Daniel rents, and that afterwards the said Tyddyn Daniel rents be applied to make up £30 to be laid out as interest for the poor for ever. Agreed also that Fenny have a lease of Tyddyn Daniel for 1 and 20 years paying yearly to the parish the sum of £10 at 2 payments, Midsummer and Christmas ....

1742   Agreed that ye Font be fixed near ye churchwarden's seat or Edward Kenrick's (one of the family lived at Pentre Mailyn and another at Stryt-yr-hwch) and that where ye said font now stands and the form adjoining now belonging to Tyddyn Daniel with ye ground appertaining to ye same from henceforth appropriated to ye use of ye present Rector's family and his successors for ever ... ye tenant of Tyddyn Daniel shall sitt in ye warden's seat or ye gallery for ye future.

1744 We the parishioners do agree and consent that Mr Anwyl shall have and make what use he pleases with the plants that are sawed at Marchwiell, which timber was fallen off Tyddyn Daniel, upon condition that he will not fell any timber down for any private uses whatsoever without free consent of the parish.

1752 Agreed that a Clock be bought for ye use of ye Church. A Church ley (levy) of 1d per pound to be levied on the inhabitants.

Despite these interim repairs it appears that it was decided in about 1773 to rebuild the church entirely .

1773 9d in the pound to be raised towards the rebuilding of the said church.

November 1773 agreed that the church be new pewed according to the plan produced by Wm. Worrall; the old pew materials to be used as far as they shall go and the fronts to be new and uniform, the flooring to be of oak and Worrall agrees to be paid by the yard.

Maurice Anwyl (Rector)   John Edwards (Curate)
John Caesar & James Palin (Churchwardens)

The name of Philip Yorke appears in the book for the first time at this point; he had been made a churchwarden at Easter 1773 and is stated to be 'of Sontley', meaning New Sontley, which he had recently bought. A paper in the Erddig collection refers to a dispute concerning his share in a pew, with testimony given to the Clerk on 22 October 1772 by Mrs Elizabeth Wright. She had been a servant of John Meller at Erddig in 1723, she then marrying Matthew Wright who leased Stryt-yr-Hwch, and William Jones always sat next to them. Jonathan Moor, grandson of Mr John Erthig, sat there for 3 years making 86 years in all. She clearly felt that this gave the Yorke family and its tenants an indisputable claim.

An undated document which must have been drawn up not later than 1774 reads as follows:

We whose names are hereunto subscribed Do promise to contribute towards repairing and improving the Parish Church of Marchwiel in the County of Denbigh and to pay the respective sums of money set down opposite to our respective names

Maurice Anwyl, Rector of Marchwiel	£50	0s	0d
Philip Yorke	£30	0s	0d
Dorothy Yorke (his mother)	£20	0s	0d
Charles Browne	£50	0s	0d
Wm. Lloyd of Plaspower Esq	£10	10s	0d

1774 Agreed that Worrall shall build a gallery according to the plan delivered, for the sum of £57. Mr Ellis, Mr Browne and Mr Edgworth have agreed to pay the said £57, and they are to sell as many pews in the gallery as will repay them.

17th March 1774 Agreed that Rev Mr Anwyl will advance Worrall £25 in part of his demand for the reading and clerk's desk and pulpit erected in the church; the parishioners to repay the £25 within 6 months. To help to discharge the debt for the

Gallery, 5 pews in it are to be sold by public auction at the Clerk's house at prices between £5 and £25, Worrall to be present with the price of erecting each pew. The first pew under the gallery was purchased by Chas. Browne Esq, and the rest auctioned later. (Several of the brass nameplates from these pews are now displayed at the back of the church, including that of the Yorkes of Erddig; we must remember that these were box pews to accommodate a whole family and its servants, and they were not removed until the church was refurbished in the 1920s.)

July 14th 1774 Whereas the ancient gallery was originally built from the rents of Tyddyn Daniel for the use of the inhabitants who had no seats in the church, it is ordered that the modern gallery be also applied to the same purpose. The seat below the gallery, through which there is a passage to the tower, shall be applied to the use of the Parish Officers who are 8 in number viz. 2 Churchwardens and Overseers of the Poor, 3 Surveyors of the Highways and 3 Constables — and it is further ordered that Worrall do make a decent cover of oak to the font, the old one being decayed ... The account with Worrall stands thus:

The total for building the Church and inside work — £370 18s 11d
He has received from various sources, mainly subscriptions, £325 10s 0d
He is still owed £150 8s 11d. A ley to be collected to repay Mr Yorke's £40. Parish debt due — £10 8s 11d

Further leys and mortgages on Tyddyn Daniel were raised in 1774, and it is clear that the main work on the church was done in that year, so that the reference to 1778 on the window inscription remains a puzzle; probably it means that all debts were cleared by that time. At the same period, however, it was realised that the parish had been exceeding the terms of its arrangement over Tyddyn Daniel, for in July 1774 '... it is further ordered that there be a ley raised on the parish for Bread and Wine, Washing, Registering, Bell ringing, Clock winding and Church necessaries all which for a time past most wrongfully was deducted out of the rent of Tyddyn Daniel'. This decision was signed by Mr Anwyl and his churchwarden, William Youd, and also by Philip Yorke and Charles Browne, the two most generous supporters of rebuilding.

William Worrall, of whom we have heard much here, was the mason who also refaced the West Front of Erddig with stone blocks; the walls of the new church do call to mind the West wall of the Yorkes' home, and both projects were completed in the 1770s. In fact the new tower was not built until 1789 at the expense of Mr Yorke (Mr Browne of Marchwiel Hall contributing £50).

One other reference to the building occurs in the early 1770s when the first Philip Yorke had become a regular attender and churchwarden. His neighbour at Plas Grono, Charles Apperley, writing as 'Nimrod' forty years after Philip's death, tells the following story about the last years of the old church or the early days of the new one, bearing in mind that the nave was rebuilt first, then the chancel and lastly, in about 1789, the tower:

Marchwiel Church 1816. From a drawing by Moses Griffith.   *[National Library of Wales]*

... He was sitting in Marchwiel Church with his back to an old gentleman who had falled asleep in the sermon, when one of his tremendous sneezes exploded. Now it happened that some doubt existed at the time as to the stability of the tower ... which was about to be repaired; and the old gentleman, imagining that the noise ... was caused by its fall, absolutely tumbled to the ground with affright, and being in a weak state of health at the time, it was said he never recovered it. Mr Yorke used to say he believed he was the only man who had ever sneezed another to death.

In 1823 the churchyard was enlarged and enclosed with a stone wall and iron railing, again using Tyddyn Daniel rents; the vestry meetings in that year were very much involved with costings and dealings with the commissioners for the new Turnpike road which passed the church. Penson, the surveyor, (who had also surveyed the new road) charged the wardens five guineas for his plans and the total cost of the project was £348 10s 9d. Tyddyn Daniel timber and rents again met most of that coSt In that year too, the first female churchwarden, Elizabeth Jones of the Woodhouse, had been appointed. In 1828 Simon Yorke Esq of Erddig, Philip's son, became a Trustee and plans went ahead to raise a sum not exceeding £200 on the property, in order to enlarge the church with the erection of a North Transept. Rector Luxmoore gave £100 and the plans and contract for the new extension were drawn up by Edward Jones at a cost of £17 12s, the final bill being £411 11s 0d. This development, however, was not a universally popular decision, as the following letter indicates; it was written by a local farmer to Mr Yorke's agent, Mr Hughes, in 1828, and we can reasonably assume that he spoke for many in the parish.

Shall I beg of you if you Please to ask Esqr.York wether his tennants must submit to the Rector for to have the Church made bigger or not. There is a many of the parishioners as thinks the Church is Big enuff for the People in the Parish. There is gone out of the Poor Rate since Tyddyn Daniel has been mortgaged this last time nearly £60. And that causes the Poor Rates to be higher than what they should be. By the Rector's Discourse I should think that Esqr. York is agreable to it. If he is not agreable to it, I am assured his tenants will not hold to have it done. Mr Hughes, I ask your pardon for troubling you, and I hope that Esqr. Yorke will not take it amiss of me for mentioning it. I would have come to Erthig myself only I am busy sowing. I would thank you for Answer if you have opportunity to give me one.

I am your most obedient servant.

Edward Jones the builder was not entirely happy either. It appears that the memorial to Philip Yorke I was originally further down the North wall than at present, and his son Simon, on realising that in order to build the North Transept the whole thing would have to be moved, employed his estate workers to do the work. The builder had already arranged that his men would carry out the removal at a cost of no more than 12 shillings, and presumably felt that the vestry should not be asked to pay the Erddig staff. The outcome is not known.

This period of improvements continued for a while longer, the tenant of Tyddyn Daniel at this time being one William Bradshaw; he was always given dinner when he came to pay his rent, and the Trustees claimed the cost of half a crown. In 1829, however, Bradshaw was given notice to quit and the tenancy was offered to Edward Davies at an increased rent of £42 per annum. In 1832 again the rents of Tyddyn Daniel were used:

To painting the Transept 5 times in oil	£9 10s
To painting the North Side once	£1 5s
To retouching the Arch	5s

In 1833 Mr Luxmoore offered personally to defray the cost of altering the pews in order to provide 40 free seats for children and others, leaving only a one shilling levy on the parish, and his offer was thankfully accepted by the vestry, no doubt bearing in mind the recent discontent about spending. It was also agreed that 'the trelice windows of the Tower of the church be painted thrice in oils, stone colour'.

In 1891 a heating system was installed for the first time in the church, and the final £30 of the cost was met from the rents of Tyddyn Daniel. Its economic importance to Rectors and churchwardens in the eighteenth and nineteenth centuries is quite clear from these details, and indeed the church still benefits indirectly; when the property was sold to its tenant, Mr Charles Clutton, in the 1920s, the proceeds were invested by the Church in Wales and make it possible for financial assistance to continue when necessary.

List of the known Rectors of Marchwiel

1359 Llewelyn Llogell Rhyson.

1399 William Sprotford.

1403 Iorwerth ap Ednyfed ap Gruffudd.

1404 Matthew ap David, clerk, collated to Marchweayl, void (vacant) because the late Iorwerth ... held it for a year or more without having himself ordained priest and without dispensation Papal Letter from Pope Boniface IX to John Trevor, Bishop of St Asaph.

1439 Roger Bolton.

1488 David ap huysskin.

1530 John ap David 'In the book of the Vicar General of the Bishop of London, 18th Jan *1530/31* he is Rector of St Olave, Silver Street, London, in addition to which he holds the livings of Wharrwhele (Marchwiel?) diocese of St Asaph, and Drayton, diocese of Coventry & Lichfield.

1536 Wilhelmus Lewys, Rect. de Merthwely. Denied the Papal Supremacy.

1537 Sir William Kay (or Key).

1540 David ap Edward (Vicar of Ruabon 1539, deprived); Rector of Llandegla 1556.

1556 Hugh de Sontley, 4th son of Robert Wyn Sonlli of Sonlli in this parish (Vicar of Wrexham in 1566).

1598 Peter Williams, AM; Vicar of Ruabon 1600.

1614 Richard Lloyd, DD, Canon 1617 (Vicar of Ruabon 1617-46. Deprived by Parliamentary Sequestrators).

1641 *John Lloyd (son of the above). A brother of Bishop Lloyd of Bangor.

1668 *Joseph Hanmer, DD.

1691 Thomas Smith (or Smythe), BD, Fellow of Jesus College, Oxford.

1709 *Humphrey Ffoulkes, MA, DD, Jesus College, Oxford.

1737 *Maurice Anwyl (Vicar of Hope 1731).

1775 Samuel Strong, MA, Trinity College Cambridge. Canon 1798.

1816 Charles Thomas Corindon Luxmoore, MA.

1824 *John Henry Montagu Luxmoore, MA (cousin of the above); produced a bilingual 'Instruction in the Fasts and Festivals of the Church' — the Welsh by Rev Evan Evans of Llanarmon.

1860 Stephen Donne MA, St John's College, Cambridge. His son William Donne MA was an Hon. Chaplain to King Edward VII.

1867 William Henry Boscawen, BA, Magdalen Hall, Oxford.

1882 *John Sturkey, BD, St David's College Lampeter.

1895 *Enoch Rhys James, BD, St David's College, Lampeter.

1901 *David Jones, BA, St David's College, Lampeter. Canon 1897.

1903 Griffith Jones, St Bees. Canon 1897.

1907 William Henry Fletcher, MA, Christ Church, Oxford (Vicar of Wrexham 1891–1906).

1926 *Evan Edward Thomas, MA, DLitt (Wales, Jena and Heidelburg); Canon 1949 (Chancellor of St Asaph 1954).

1964 David Saunders Davies, BA Lampeter.

1975 Tegid O Jones, LlB; from 1983 Rector of Marchwiel and Isycoed. Rural Dean 1986.

1993 David A Slim, Chancellor's Scholar, the Bishop's Hostel, Lincoln Theological College. Rector of the Grouped Benefice of Marchwiel and Isycoed.

This list of incumbents reflects quite clearly the religious upheavals of the Tudor and Stuart periods. Indeed even earlier, in 1403, Iorwerth ap Ednyfed became rector, only to be deprived a year later because he had not been ordained and had no papal dispensation. In 1530 John ap David was clearly guilty of pluralism, apparently holding three livings, while in 1539 David ap Edward was deprived of the living of Ruabon, only to become Rector of Marchwiel a year later. We can only assume that he refused to take the Oath of Supremacy demanded by Henry VIII, but how he managed to be re-instated remains a mystery. Then there is the case of Dr Richard Lloyd, who became Rector in 1614; in 1642 his name appeared on a list of

* denotes burial in the churchyard

'orthodox divines' suitable for giving instruction and counsel in Church reform and submitted by Parliament. Yet in 1641, just before the outbreak of the Civil War, he was replaced in Marchwiel by his son and in 1646, in the middle of the war, he was deprived of the living of Ruabon by the Parliamentary Sequestrators. It would be interesting to know more about the reasons for the decline in his career prospects; evidently this did not affect his two sons, since one followed him in Marchwiel while another became Bishop of Bangor.

The family had very close links with Sir Thomas Myddelton of Chirk, MP for Denbighshire and a leading Parliamentary figure — indeed in 1639 Richard Lloyd became tutor to the Myddelton children and his nephew on his wife's side, Rev Michael Hughes, became Vicar of Chirk. John Lloyd, the son who succeeded his father at Marchwiel, was obviously a man of many talents; among his Oxford qualifications was that of Doctor of Physic, and he became physician to the family at Chirk Castle. When Sir Thomas died in 1666, Rev John Lloyd was among the many people who were provided, according to the castle accounts, with black cloth at 21s 6d per yard to have mourning clothes made. He himself died two years later at the age of 66, and was buried in Marchwiel.

Another of his successors, Dr Humphrey Ffoulkes, was a considerable scholar and enjoyed a high reputation among his fellow clergy for his scholarly writings on theological and philosophical topics and on the history of Wales in the Middle Ages. Up to now this list of Rectors has included Rev Thomas Holland as serving between 1737 and 1749, but unfortunately these dates are not accurate; he certainly lived in Marchwiel at various times from 1722 to the 1740s, leasing the Hall at one stage, but also being described as 'of Gresford' and 'of Wrexham'. His name does appear in the Vestry Book, but only alongside that of Dr Ffoulkes, and I believe that perhaps he assisted him in the parish. Dr Ffoulkes was succeeded in 1737 by Rev Maurice Anwyl, who served the parish for nearly forty years and lived to see the rebuilt church through its first stage. Mr Anwyl died unmarried and his estate was administered by his widowed sister, Mary Ellis, who had presumably kept house for him in the Rectory which he improved and extended. In contrast to these two thoroughly Welsh priests, however, the next Rector was Rev Samuel Strong, a native of Devon who became a personal friend of Philip Yorke I and presided over the second stage of the rebuilding and refurnishing of the church at the end of the 18th century. He also was a fine scholar and had earlier been Rector of Newtown, whilst his wife, Anne George, was a Dorset heiress. He was a man of many parts; the writer 'Nimrod', Charles James Apperley of Plas Grono, summarised his personality thus:

> He was one of the best shots in the neighbourhood and enjoyed his rubber of whist, at which he generally excelled his fellows. It would appear he read his Bible, as every man should read it, without finding anything in its dictates which forbids a reasonable enjoyment of innocent pleasures, or moderate relaxation of the various

cares of life ... Mr Strong's religion was truly practical, and consisted more in the beautiful spirit of benevolence than that of any man in his station with whom I have hitherto been acquainted ... My father did not attend his own parish church, giving the preference to that of Marchwiel from the high esteem he entertained for its Rector ... The distance (from the Rectory to the Church) being little over half a mile, when the weather admitted of it he always walked, accompanied by his two daughters and his only son, if he was at home; and a most respectable and truly clerical appearance did he make. He generally wore a full cocked hat, carried a strong gold-headed cane in his hand, had somewhat of a dignified step, which gave a commanding air to his carriage; and it was delightful to see the respect paid to him by his flock. ... Strange to say, there was a strong resemblance in form and character between himself and his clerk ... On descending from the pulpit, the clerk's snuffbox was presented to the rector, who took one pinch as a refresher, we may presume, after the fatigue he had gone through. ... There was in this familiar act something characteristic of the benevolent feeling that ought to exist between two persons simultaneously engaged in the exercise of their holy calling.

There are in the chancel two memorials, one to Rector Strong and one to his wife Anne.

As has already been indicated, several of these distinguished men were laid to rest in the old churchyard; Rev Maurice Anwyl's grave is near the choir vestry window, near that of Dr Humphrey Ffoulkes, whilst Rev John Sturkey, Rev Enoch James, Rev J H M Luxmoore, Rev David Jones and Canon Thomas lie in the eastern part of the churchyard outside the chancel.

Tithes and Terriers

There is in the archives another document known as a Glebe Terrier and dated 1791; it records all the glebe land (hence the name, which is derived from the Latin 'terra") and the tithes which were payable to the church and it summarises the prosperity enjoyed by the Rectors of Marchwiel during the late Georgian period. The original spelling has been retained.

A true Terrier of all the Glebe lands, Tenements, Tythes, Portions of Tythes and other rights belonging to the Rectory and Parish Church of Marchwiel in the County of Denbigh and Diocese of St Asaph, now in the use and possession of Rev Samuel Strong there, or his tenants, taken, made and renewed according to the old evidences and the knowledge of the antient inhabitants, at a vestry holden this 11th day of June 1791 ... and exhibited in the primary visitation of the Right Rev Father in God Lewis, Lord Bishop of St Asaph, holden at Wrexham.

The Parsonage house, built of brick and covered with slates, consists of a large kitchen and Brewhouse, another kitchen, a long passage, a .... (word not clear), three pantries, a cellar, closet and two parlours. Six bedchambers, a study and one garret, the whole being in the inside about seventy feet long by forty wide, including the outer kitchen.

The Outbuildings belonging thereunto are a Barn of four bays, measuring together fifty seven feet in length by nineteen feet. Another barn of four bays, sixty one feet by eighteen feet and contiguous to this one a stable, cowhouse and another barn about seventy feet by nineteen feet. Another stable with three stalls, having granaries over it, with a pig-stye, hen roost and a small room attached to it. A cart-house and coach-house, all built of timber and brick and covered with thatch, a pigeon house built of brick and slated.

A Garden and orchard containing about half an acre, all contiguous to the house, fenced in part with quickset hedges and towards the North with about fifty yards of brick wall. There are also three courts and a farmyard, fenced with paling and walls, and containing about the eighth part of an acre. Also two closes called the pigeon house crofts, containing nearly an acre of land fenced with quickset hedges. The said building and parcels of glebeland have the Highway on the West, the lands of Philip Yorke Esq on the North and East and those of John Ellis Esq on the South side thereof. There are thirteen ash-trees, four firs, one oak and one Horse chestnut growing upon the same, besides a number of Beeches, Poplars and Firs lately planted. Value uncertain.

Glebe: An House joining to the churchyard, consisting of five bays of timber and brick building, covered with thatch and divided into four dwellings which with the gardens and a small close contain upwards of half an acre, having the Turnpike road on the South side thereof, the churchyard on the west, the lands of Chas Browne Esq on the North and those of Wm Lloyd Esq on the East.

Also a parcel of land called Erw'r Deial, having the Turnpike road on the north side thereof, the lands of Philip Yorke Esq on the other sides, containing about an acre, fenced with quicksetts'ì. (This land was later called upon, in 1874, to build the Church school which served the village for a century, until the present building off the Station Road was erected to replace it.) All these lands and tenements 'the Rector enjoys separately and entirely' with 4 other parcels of land 'which partake of the nature of glebe':

1. Part of a field called Erw Cwtt-y-defaid (one third of an acre)
2. Part of a field belonging to Philip Yorke Esq called Cae Ucha (a quarter of an acre)
3. A field called 'The Barncroft' lying near the Turnpike — about half an acre.
4. Cefn Dreiniog belonging to Mrs Ann Shackerley — half an acre.

The Rector for the time being hath nothing but common tythe from these 4 parcels of land, except when they are ploughed; then, he hath first his tythe of the whole and afterwards a third part of the Corn growing upon the said glebe. The Tythes of Corn, Hay and Things of that nature are payable in kind; throughout the parish none plead custom or prescription - the 10th sheaf of corn, the 7th lamb, accounting for three, or paying 4d a lamb - if under Seven, the owner pays 4d a lamb to the Parson. The Parson is to choose the 3rd lamb and the 3rd fleece out of every ten ... For a cow calved 1d; for a mare foaled 4d; one goose of a flock, if but 3, and only one if 30. A pig from every sow that farrows, if there be three or more. A kid of every man's flock if there be three. For hemp and flax as settled by Act of Parliamant. The tenth of apples, honey and eggs.

Easter dues: for a man and wife 5d; a widower, widow, single person, servant man or maid, 3d; a person that hath a trade 4d.

Hay, clover and rye-grass are tytheable in Grasscocks, but the Rector has for many years taken the 11th cock made into hay instead of the 10th grass cock; and usually the 11th shock or hattock or corn in lieu of the 10th sheaf.

Utensils — a silver flagon, silver chalice with a patine, silver plate or dish, and a small silver cup with a cover, having the following inscription on them: *Deo et usibus parochialis ecclesiae de Marchwiel in Com: Denbigh Testamento suo legavit Johannes Hill de Sontley Armiger AD MDCCXXXI* (John Hill of Sontley Esq bequeathed these in his will to God and for the use of the parish church of Marchwiel in the County of Denbigh AD 1731) (A note below says that the weight of the plate was, when new, 117oz 18dwt exclusive of the small cup and cover.)

One crimson velvet carpet fringed with gold, one pulpit cushion of the same with 4 golden tassels, and a pulpit cloth of the like velvet with a gold fringe, and embroidered in the front —bequeathed by the aforesaid John Hill Esq. One linen cloth and napkin for the Communion table, one black bier cloth and bier, 2 surplices and one bell weighing 5cwt 3qrs 7lbs.

Books: one large English Bible (Oxford 1727) 2 large English Common Prayer Books, Book of Homilies, 2 registers in parchment.

Funds for the repair of the Church — a tenement called Tyddyn Daniel in the Parish of Marchwiel, made over in trust for the parishioners to Philip Yorke and Chas. Browne Esq (1771) and by them leased (1787) to Richard Barker for 21 years at £21 per annum, deducting £1 0s 10d per annum for the King's rent. The walls and roof of the chancel are repaired by the owners of the pews in it; the churchyard fence by the Parishioners: no part of either lies upon the Rector.

The parish clerk, who is also the sexton, is appointed by the Rector, who pays him 40s per annum. The parishioners, by a stipend and fees, make up the rest of his salary.

Signed this 11th day of June 1791
by Samuel Strong (Rector)
Churchwardens including Richard Barker
and parishioners notably John Dunbabin

On the copy there are notes by Rev J H M Luxmoore, Rector between 1824 and 1860; the same conditions clearly applied several decades later. The document was exhibited at the visitation of Robert, the Ven Archdeacon Wickham in June 1855 and it gives us not only a full account of the way in which the tithe system worked, but also the most detailed inventory of the church's valuables two centuries ago, several of which, happily, still exist. In 1856, perhaps at the Archdeacon's request, another Terrier was drawn up and makes a useful comparison with 1791. The glebe lands were described as follows: 'adjoining the churchyard a House consisting of four bays of timber and brick building covered with thatch, measuring 24 yards by 6 yards and divided into a school (see the chapter on education) and three dwellings tenanted severally by Richard Jones, William Jones and Charles Prince. Also gardens and close making three quarters of an acre.' The dwellings on this site were known as Glebe Cottages until recent years. Mr Luxmoore's Rectory is described as 'built of brick, 23 yards by 8 yards containing hall, drawing room and dining room and north room with attics over them and a library with no attic and also offices, pantries and kitchens, also detached two stables, Coach house, cart house with granaries over, cow house, pig styes and Barn of three bays.' This description refers to the house which Mr Luxmoore had built in 1825 when he first came to Marchwiel. It is the elegant late Georgian building, now known as the Old Rectory, on Woodhouse Lane, beyond Bentleys Farm, and the architect was Thomas Penson (1790–1859), an Oswestry man who had also surveyed the new turnpike road and designed the North Transept in the church. Some of Mr Luxmoore's negotiations are mentioned in the chapter on the Yorkes; the house was sold by the Church in Wales a century later, shortly after the arrival of Dr E E Thomas as Rector in 1926, and is now in private ownership. The Rectory referred to in 1791 had been improved and extended by Rev Maurice Anwyl in his first year in the parish (1737/38) and it was visited and sketched by the North Wales artist Moses Griffith in 1816; much of it was demolished to make way for Penson's new building. The present Rectory was built on the Overton Road shortly after Dr Thomas's arrival and has been the home of the incumbent ever since.

The 1856 Terrier was witnessed at a specially convened Terrier Vestry by the Rector and churchwardens, Richard Huxley and John Davies, who had to make his mark; the rest included Simon Yorke and Richard Birch (Old Hall), John Morris (The Groves), John Parsonage (Five Fords), Ths Thomas (The Plassey), Thos. Cheetham (Tanylan) and Chas Evans (Top House).

Rector Luxmoore was a most meticulous man and he caused to be bound and preserved for the use of his successors two volumes which give us the most detailed information on all those who owned or tenanted land in both Marchwiel and Sontley. When we look at the amount of tithes in kind which Rectors like Rev Samuel Strong received, we are not surprised that he was very content with his situation, but in 1836 the system which had persisted for almost a thousand years was radically altered, after years of complaint and discontent; tithes were commuted by the Whig government into a money payment or tithe-rent. Mr Luxmoore wrote a sorrowful preface to his books of valuations, as follows:

> I have caused these Tythe accounts to be thus richly bound that they might be preserved by my successors, the Rectors of Marchwiel and that some memorandum might exist exhibiting the liberality and judicious arrangements of our Ancestors in their endowments of the Church: and I hereby testify that it is with the unanimous regret of all parties, whether Tythe owner, landowners or tenants that Tythes are this

day extinct. The existence of Tythes as arranged in this parish was advantageous to all, since when the LORD of the Harvest gave rich crops, the tenant was enabled to pay accordingly, and when the crops were light, or when the Tenant anticipated any difficulty in paying at Christmas the amount of them, he had the option of taking or refusing his Tythes, and such good understanding existed between the Tythe owner and tenant that I have frequently known the tenant offer to take his Tythes to the Rectory gratuitously. Therefore it was to the regret of all parties that in the parish of Marchwiel Tythes ceased on the feast of Circumcision 1842.

J H Montagu Luxmoore, Rector
Feast of Epiphany 1842

A note below this Preface states that the average value of tithes over the last ten years, 1830–40, was £683, whilst the commutation value, *ie* the total rents in lieu, came to only £636. Each person occupying land is recorded on a double page, Great Tithes on the left and Small Tithes on the right. Payment was made per acre of wheat, barley, oats, peas, beans and vetches. Small tithes included those on potatoes, turnips, cows and calves, farrow cows, lambs, wool and colts, hemp and flax, and finally Easter dues and hay and corn tithes.

We also have details of the menu for the farmers' dinner which about thirty attended on February 7th 1837; it included boiled beef, plum pudding, goose, tarts, ham, turkey and roast beef. We are assured that there was no second course — except butter, cheese, celery, salad etc! Tithes continued to be a fact of rural life, in the form of tithe rents, for another century, in fact as late as 1936, and in many Nonconformist areas caused great offence, though no trouble is recorded in Marchwiel.

The Census of 1851 included a separate return from churches and chapels up and down the country, and the population of the village in that year was declared to be 237 males and 216 females. Seats in the church — free, 114; others, 155. At morning service there were 98 people and 54 scholars; in the evening only 19 and 50 scholars. (Many churches added on their returns the fact that the poor weather on the day of the census, March 30th, had brought about the lower than average attendance). The tithe was said to yield £614 3s 0d and the glebe was still about 3 acres with 4 cottages, with a value of £50 per year. The Rectory was rated at £12 6s 8d and we find that the church had to find £20 a year for the curate and make a contribution of £42 towards the school. (The first National School had been established in what is now Old Rectory or Woodhouse Lane in 1826.)

The Church Interior

The present building was quite possibly intended to be cruciform in shape, with a South Transept to balance the North, but this never came about. It has been suggested that as the tower calls to mind the tradition of Sir Christopher Wren's London churches, with its balustre parapet and four weathercocks, the great man may have been asked to design it; there is a belief that he was staying at Wynnstay Hall in 1709 when the two churchwardens (one of them was Jos Edisbury)were paid 6d by the vestry 'for their journey to Ruabon', but much though we should like to accept this theory, there is unfortunately no other evidence; in any case Wren died in 1723, some time before the rebuilding.

The altar was, until earlier this century, a marble slab, but in 1927 it was replaced by a carved wooden table and reredos in memory of Canon Fletcher and paid for by the parishioners; its predecessor was given Eyton church in 1928. The three-sided apse has windows commemorating, on the left of the altar Simon Yorke (died 1834 aged 63) and on the right his wife Margaret (died 1848 aged 70). The centre window was originally presented by Mr Mainwaring of Marchwiel Hall to mark the births of his three children. A window in the nave, illustrating the Good Samaritan, is in memory of the Rev J H M Luxmoore '36 years Rector of this parish', 1860.

Perhaps the best known feature of the nave is the Yorke window on the South wall; it is placed very close to the position of the family vault outside and beneath the church and it contains 18 shields and four crests relating to not only the Yorkes, but also the Edisburys and Custs of Erddig. It commemorates not merely the family but also the completion of the rebuilding of the church in the 1770s. Young Simon Yorke wrote from school at Eton to his father (Philip I) on September 30 1787:

> I hope I shall find (the window) up by Christmas, as I think it will be a great ornament to the church and be well approved of by those who see it, for the arms which Mr Eggleton has painted....

The whole wall is taken up with the family's memorial tablets: on the left of the window is one commemorating the first Simon — 'a pious, temperate country gentleman, of a very mild, just and benevolent character, as the concern for his death did best testify'. On the same side is the marble monument to his daughter Anne Jemima Yorke, who died in 1770 aged 16; it depicts a drooping figure above a serpent coiled around a rose, in a possible reference to the tuberculosis which killed her in the bloom of youth. It was erected by 'her disconsolate mother' and Thomas Pennant noted it on his visit to Marchwiel in the late 1770s — 'a small elegant monument in memory of Miss Yorke of Erddig, who ... opening into bloom, was snatched away in 1770'. Next to this is a splendid sculpture said to be by Pieter Scheemakers in memory of John Meller Esq (*Iohannis Meller, Armiger*) who died in 1733 and was the first of the family at Erddig to be buried in Marchwiel. On the opposite wall is a marble of a female figure mourning over an unstrung harp; this commemorates Anne Jemima's brother, Philip Yorke I, author of *The Royal Tribes of Wales*, who died in 1804 aged 61; by 1805 his son Simon (the one who had been so pleased with the window) had commissioned the work from Richard Westmacott, who wrote from London apologising for the delay and explaining that he was working on a national monument at the same time, in addition to standing for election as an Associate of the Royal Academy; the completed design arrived soon afterwards. Philip I's first wife Elizabeth, daughter of Sir John Cust, Speaker of the House of Commons in two of King George III's parliaments, is also remembered. Further along the same wall is the memorial to Mr Edgeworth and his family of Bryn-y-grog.

Perhaps one of the most poignant of all the Yorke memorials can be seen to the side of the pulpit, commemorating the last squire of Erddig, Philip Yorke III, who died in 1978 five years after bequeathing his whole property to the nation through the National Trust. His funeral service was one of the most memorable events in the church's recent history and it was the Trust which erected the memorial.

Among the other plaques is one behind the clergy desk, in remembrance of another of the Yorkes, Lieut Victor Yorke, of the Royal Engineers, younger son of Simon Yorke III, who was killed by Basuto pickets in 1881 and buried in Palmersfontein, South Africa. A brass behind the lectern commemorates Captain Ellis of Eyton Villa, a most generous benefactor, who left £5,000 to the parish when he died in 1858. Next to it a tablet remembers Gerald Piercy, grandson of Benjamin Piercy, who continued his grandfather's links with Sardinia and was killed in a road accident there.

The octagonal font was presented by Mr S P Hope of Marchwiel Hall. (We have no description of its predecessor, but a vestry note of December 1742 confirmed that the area near the font of that time 'be from henceforth appropriated to ye use of ye present Rector's family and his successors for ever and wee whose names are underwritten do Impower ye Rector to erect a seat on ye aforesaid premises when he pleases'. Signed: Roger Roberts and Richard Owens). Mr Hope was succeeded at the Hall by the Piercy family, who were also generous in their gifts to the church, school and village, and after Mr Benjamin Piercy's death in 1888 his widow presented the pipe organ in his memory; it was installed in the tower gallery in 1909, displacing the seats and harmonium which had previously occupied the space. Powered by electricity since 1934, it makes a fine addition to a small country church, despite being in urgent need of restoration (1997). The very distinctive peal of bells was installed in 1930 to replace the existing single one, which was recast to make the new No. 5 bell. The dedication was performed by the Archbishop of Wales and the commemorative plaque unveiled by Mrs McAlpine.

The present church clock, with its black face and gilded figures, was installed by Messrs Joyce and Co. of Whitchurch in August 1892 at a cost of £80 and has been a landmark, in sight and sound, ever since, with only two or three interruptions for maintenance and re-gilding.

When the North Transept was built in 1829, it included a gallery for a small organ, which was used throughout the nineteenth century until displaced by the new one under the tower. This earlier instrument was a barrel-organ which automatically, at the turn of a handle, played several hymn tunes. If restored it would have been a fine museum piece, but sad to say, it was left to deteriorate and has now disappeared. Also now removed, but this time to its proper resting place, is the base and part of the shaft of a stone cross which is said to date from the 14th century and to have been found 'in the bulwark of the river about two furlongs from the church of Bangor Monachorum, 1849' according to the brass plate fixed to it. It was rescued by Mr Luxmoore and remained in the Rectory garden for safe keeping for almost a century before being placed at the foot of the lectern in the 1950s, at the instigation of Canon Thomas. It has now been moved again, to its rightful home in Bangor. An article in the *Wrexham Leader* in 1968 referring to the cross provoked an unexpected reaction — a letter from New Zealand. It came from Mr Arthur Griffith Jones, son of Canon Griffith Jones, the Rector appointed in 1903. He remembered the cross in the Rectory garden; indeed he went on to say that it was mounted on some stones which he once climbed as a child while playing, and dislodged the monument, so that it came rolling to the ground, narrowly missing his baby sister.

The interior of the church was completely refurbished in the 1920s, when the box pews were removed (much to the distress of the Yorke family) and the pulpit replaced with the present one given in memory of Mrs Piercy of Marchwiel Hall, by her son and daughters. The Litany desk was presented by Mr Acton of Wrexham and the new choir stalls by Mrs David Roberts of Grove Cottage, in memory of her husband. The oil lamps of early photographs were replaced in 1934 with electric lights as soon as the supply became available in the village. A further major project was planned in the 1930s and designs were submitted, but the coming of war in 1939 put a stop to the idea. The architects' report may be of interest:

> The church, though relatively small, possesses unusual interest ... Its special claim to be valued lies in the fact that it is in the tradition of ecclesiastical architecture initiated by Sir Christopher Wren. It is an early authentic example of that quiet and seemly manner of design which was devised specifically to meet the needs of the Protestant religion and which satisfied and continues to satisfy them in a peculiarly appropriate degree. The simplicity of the plan, the pleasant shape and proportions of the tower and nave, the repose and dignity of the main congregational space, with its terminal arches and its rhythmic order of high windows combine to constitute a work that is distinguished by fitness, sobriety and beauty.

After the arrival of Dr and Mrs Thomas in 1926, it became the custom to hold regular church socials to pay for such items as cleaning and redecoration, and local bands were hired for these occasions. By 1935 there had been female voices in the choir for some time, and it was decided to buy their first purple gowns. Since 1912 the organist and choirmaster had been the Headmaster, Mr Hunt, but he was obliged in 1934 to resign the position through ill health, and Mr Rupert Matthias was in due course appointed. He was succeeded in 1939 by Mr Walter Oliver, who served the church for almost forty years.

To return to the church's appearance, the most recent additions to the North

Marchwiel Church— artists sketch of the pulpit. possibly installed about 1778 and removed in the 1920s. {Sybil Wynne Jones]

Transept are the painting in the style of Andrea del Sarto entitled Disputation over the Sacraments (presented in the 1950s in memory of Mr and Mrs Greenwood of Bryn-y-grog) and a modern stained glass window, traditional in style, commemorating Mr C D Jenkins, who died in 1985 having given many years of devoted and generous service to the church and village as well as to the Maelor Hospital in Wrexham. The fine processional cross was presented by Mrs A M J Thomas in memory of her husband, Canon E E Thomas who was Rector for very nearly forty years and died in 1964.

In the 1960s the church was scheduled as a building of historic and architectural interest, but unfortunately a comprehensive report of 1967 warned that much of the woodwork and stonework of the nave and tower was in need of immediate attention because of the ravages of time and death-watch beetle. A Restoration Fund was established and as a result the building was safeguarded whilst at the same time the pews were removed from the North Transept and replaced with chairs to facilitate meetings other than services; the whole aisle was carpeted, and lighting and heating were updated. Finally the window in the choir vestry was replaced, although the new clear glass has dispersed the slightly mysterious effect created by the previous tinted and opaque variety. It is interesting to note that the old window had needed urgent repairs in 1927, so that the organ could be properly tuned, and nearly seventy years later the same problem had to be dealt with.

Marchwiel Church Choir c1908. Middle row setaed (L–R): *Lizzie Williams (Mrs Pierce), ? , ? , Polly Williams (Mrs George Jones), Ena Green, Katie Jones (Mrs Pugh), Jennie Jones (Mrs Nadin).* Standing, extreme right: *May Dutton (Mrs Charles Clutton). The two boys framed in the church door are Charlie and Alfred Williams, brothers of Polly.* [A G Jones]

It is to be hoped that this history of the church demonstrates that recent changes are only the latest in a long series of alterations and improvements which have enabled St Marcella's to meet the needs of its time as it has done for many centuries.

2: The Village in the Middle Ages

The whole area around Marchwiel could be regarded as characteristically border country from the beginning of the Anglo-Saxon period, especially when in the ninth century Offa, King of Mercia, constructed the great dyke which still bears his name and which was intended to act as a boundary mark and to deter raiders from both sides. In what was known until 1974 as East Denbighshire it stopped short of the higher contours, and South of Wrexham nothing above 500 feet was occupied, but the Dyke ran right through Maelor a few miles west of Marchwiel leaving little to the Welsh but moor and mountain. For about three hundred years after Offa, the wave of settlement flowed usually from east to west, leaving, as Professor Dodd has said in his article on Welsh and English in East Denbighshire, 'some permanent deposit to enrich the variegated life of the neighbourhood'; by the time William the Conqueror had ordered Domesday Book to be compiled in 1086, all that his surveyors could include as part of his territory was a narrow strip along the rivers Dee and Alun, including the townships of Sesswick and Eyton; all the rest of the area between the Dee and the Dyke had reverted to the Welsh. Probably they were joined by Welsh tribes from the Vale of Clwyd and elsewhere, and were not opposed by the Mercian (*ie* English) inhabitants, who found them better neighbours than the Normans. A process of assimilation went on until by the thirteenth century there were hardly more than a dozen English names among the tenants of Wrexham and none in the other Mercian settlements, presumably including Marchwiel. Welsh law was enforced and Welsh tribal customs prevailed, this period marking the height of the power of the Welsh princes.

Two of the new arrivals referred to above were the Elidyr and Kenrick groups who in the late eleventh century had swept down from the hills south of Llandegla and beyond Esclusham Mountain, to settle on the fertile farmland near the Dee. Politically, however, the Normans held the advantage after the death in the last quarter of the thirteenth century of Madoc ap Gruffydd, who had ruled Welsh Maelor, leaving two young sons under English guardianship. King Edward I seized the opportunity to assert his rights as overlord and granted Maelor, as part of the new lordship of Bromfield and Yale, to John de Warrenne, Earl of Surrey and guardian of the two young princes who had just died, in about 1282, in suspiciously convenient circumstances. The officers of this new lordship held monthly courts in Wrexham, with both legal and administrative functions, and court records show that despite their Norman pedigree, the courts used jurors who were always thoroughly Welsh in name, while Welsh customs were recognised and respected. The records for the year 1339-40 show that there were still very few Englishmen living in the district, which included Marchwiel, Sontley, Eyton and Erddig; indeed the trial of one such man had to be adjourned because there were not enough of his countrymen present to form a jury. In the same record we find the names of ancestors of the Broughtons of Marchwiel Hall and the Sontleys of Sontley, two families who later played a most prominent part in village and county history. Regular appearances were also made by two of the famous three bardic brothers of Marchwiel, Llewelyn, the first recorded Rector, and his brother Ednyfed.

A few years previous to this, on Tuesday May 6th 1315 to be precise, a Survey was conducted in Marchwiel by one Lord Thomas of Sheffield as part of the 'First Extent of Bromfield and Yale', which was an attempt to assess the area for the benefit of its new lord, John de Warrenne. This survey is the oldest extant work of its kind relating to any part of Wales. Why 1315? The answer must be that King Edward I, the 'Hammer of the Scots', had died leaving his task unfinished and his successor, Edward II was still locked in combat with Robert the Bruce of Scotland and in desperate need of men and money to continue his campaign, especially after his disastrous defeat at Bannockburn; clearly he needed details of the potential resources available and he was to demand 200 soldiers from the Lord of Bromfield and Yale. Marchwiel's place in the survey is recorded in a way which in just a few lines describes life under the feudal system, with details of all the dues payable — even on family and moral matters — to the Anglo-Norman establishment.

> Extent of the lands and tenements which Madoc ap Llewelyn, Hywel ap Griffith, Hywel ap Eigon, Ken... his brother, Eigon..., Hywel ap Ken...., Ken... and Eigon his brothers, Ior... ap Cadwgan, Hwfa ap Hywel, David ap Hywel, Hywel Bychan, Madoc ap Hywel and Ienna ap Ior... hold in Dinhinlle, Sesswick, Dutton Diffaeth, Dutton y Brain, Gry.....(illegible), Cacca Dutton, Allington, Hoseley, MARCHWIEL and Eyton, and render and do all services as they used to do for ... acres of land in Henlynton (Hewlington near Holt) which the lord has from them in exchange, namely 9s 5d at Martinmas and 3s 1d at Michaelmas. And they render annually at Michaelmas seven and seven twelfth bushels, worth 12d per bushel, according to the Wrexham measure ... .
>
> ... Also they pay 7s 6d, each of them, by way of relief after the death of their ancestors. Also whenever a daughter of theirs shall marry or be led astray while unmarried by different men they pay 20s. Also they are bound to go to war with the lord in England, Scotland and Wales with the body of the Earl at the cost of the said Earl, and they remain with the Earl at his will, and each of them gives for his share of £20 10s., which is paid in gross at Martinmas for the pannage (the right to let pigs feed in woodland) of free men and their tenants of Bromfield. Also all their tenants who hold houses pay, that is each of them for himself, 1½d. at Michaelmas for gathering nuts. Also they come to the court of Wrexham or Marford whenever it is proclaimed. Also each of them gives for his own share towards the making of a hall, chamber and cookhouse and the new mill at Wrexham, and this with thatching with straw. And they turn the water at the lord's mill, namely those who remain within the bailiwick of Wrexham.

The men of Sontley were also assessed in this way:

> Ior ap Griffri, Eigon ap Griffri, Ken. ap Griffri hold one messuage, 9 acres of land by estimate, and render 8½d annually at Michaelmas ... And all the tenants of the aforesaid co-sharers who have houses in which there is smoke give each of them 1½d for gathering nuts at Michaelmas ... .

One of Marchwiel's claims to fame in the fourteenth century was the great Eisteddfod which was allegedly held in about 1350, under the patronage of Lord Mortimer of Chirk; its main purpose was to regenerate Welsh poetry, which was suffering after the conquest of Wales in 1282, because the disappearance of the

Welsh princes meant the end of support for the bards. Our main source of information on the matter is the eighteenth century antiquarian Iolo Morgannwg, who rarely reveals his own sources, but it would be good to believe his story, and factual or not, it is still worth recording. The tale hinges on the role played by the three brothers of Marchwiel, the sons of Gruffydd ap Iorwerth, Lord of Sonlli and Eyton Uchaf and his wife Gwenhwyfar ferch Madog. Llywelyn, the priest, is said to have composed the englynion (verses) 'Marchwiail bedw briglas' (Marchwiel, the branched birch-tree) in the ancient style of poetry. His brother Madog, known as Madog Benfras, won a chair and a birch wreath for his poem to a lady, 'whereupon Dafydd ap Gwilym sang kindly of him for that poem'. He is known to have lived between 1300 and 1350 and his work can be seen in manuscript at the National Library of Wales. The eldest of the three was Ednyfed ap Gruffydd who succeeded his father as Lord of Sonlli and Eyton Uchaf. In addition to their literary interests, Ednyfed and Madoc often appeared at the court of the bailiwick of Wrexham as plaintiffs; on one occasion David ap Howel trespassed and cut twigs upon their land and was fined 12 pence, while on another, Madoc sued Einion ap David for one measure of corn, and won his case. Their mother Gwenhwyfar also appeared once in court, to declare herself indebted to Stephen of the Green for the sum of 29s 2d.

The earliest of all the land transactions involving Marchwiel also dates from this period, and can be found among the papers of Sir John Trevor of Plas Teg and Trevalyn. On 10 January 1341/42 Ieuan, son of David Voel, transferred to Yorwerth son of Yorwerth vap Llewelyn his lands 'between the King's Highway (New Mills to Pykhill) and the waters of Clewedoc ... and others in Marchoeil'. The witnesses were Yor. ap Eignion Duy (Du — Black), Madoc his son, Madoc Duy ap Gruffudd ap Yor., David his brother, Eignion Gogh ap David Voel and Morgan ap Iorwerth ap Lewelin'.

There are one or two other deeds which are also worth quoting:

1475 Between John Eyton of Eyton and Elys son of Elys Eyton 'settlement of lands in Bromfield to the use of the said Elys son of Elys Eyton, namely a tenement in the parish of Marchweill and one parcel of Land in Bedwell'.

1488 Extract from the will of Elys ap Elys ... to David ap huysskin, clerk, rector of the parish church of Marchwyaill, Madoc ap Iolyn Decka and David ap Yolyn ap Ievan Decka, to re-enfeoff my daughter, Margaret in all the lands which I formerly confirmed to them.

1517/18 Elis ap Richard ap Hoell granted Robert ap Edward ap Madoc a tenement and lands in the township of Marchwiell.

1550 Elis ap Richard of Alrey, Gentleman granted William Tona of Marchwiell, yeoman, land being half a meadow called Dol John Eyton in the township of Marchwiell, near the river Clowedog and Gwern y Ffynnon.

When we study the fourteenth and fifteenth centuries we are plunged into the intricacies of the feudal system at its height;the various parts of Marchwiel and its neighbouring township, Sontley, still the most rural part of the parish, were owned by just a few families of free men, most of them inter-related. The present Prince of Wales once remarked that any self-respecting herald could prove that anyone was descended from anyone if he really tried, and it is perhaps not helpful to go into all these details without more real evidence. We do know that in 1467 Commissioners met at Holt Castle on the orders of the Lord of Bromfield and Yale, and many Statutes and Ordinances were put into effect, including laws on such matters as the apprehending of vagabonds, the carrying of weapons, letters of safe conduct, taxation matters etc. One of the provisions mentioned one Eignon Gough (or Goch — the Red) de Marchwiell — 'of the ville of Marchwiell'. These feudal conditions continued until a further survey was carried out in 1620 for the benefit of Charles, Prince of Wales. (Norden's Survey of Bromfield and Yale).

> Item, there belongeth out of ye townshipp of Marchwiail and other townshipps as followeth, unto ye manor of Rhiwabon, viz, Tenementes of freeholde lands and tenementes of lease or customarie landes from the townshipp of Rhwyton.

The following is a list of free tenants which appears in the survey:

1. Emanuel Reignolds, tenet (holds) Redmor, alias Gwern Moor in Marchwiail — 20 acres
2. Robert ap Harri tenet in Marchwiail — 10 acres
3. Henricus Edgbury *ditto* —10 acres
4. Johannes Wm. Edgbury *ditto* — 2 acres
5. Oliverus Payne *ditto* — 9 acres
6. Johannes Kenrick generosus — 40 acres
7. Kenricus Dunbabin de Marchwiail — 9 acres
8. Rogerus Griffith tenet Kae Broom — 2 acres, 2 roods
9. Rosa Gruffith tenet in Marchwiail — 7 acres
10. Rogerus Jones tenet septem parcellas terr 'in Marchwiail vocat' Kae Einion y Coed, Cae Einion y Pwll, Erw Hir, Cefn Dreiniog, Erw Wrexham Y Ddol Vaes et Kae Ithel.
11. Rogerus Ellis, armiger, (Esquire) tenet in Marchwiail 100 acres
12. Ed. Meredith, draper et civis London, tenet un 'tenementum in Marchwiail et undecem
    parcellas terr' — 12 acres.
13. Idem Ed. Meredith tenet una tenementum in Marchwiail et septem clausur' vocat' 'P'.
    no'ia de Kae Uchaf, Kae yr Yskiber, Y Tir Newydd, Erw Bryn y Grog, Gwern y Ffynnon, y Kae Isaf et Erw wrth y Ty — 12 acres.
14. Blanch Carden (corrected to Roger Powell) tenet in Marchwiail — 2 acres.

Several of these surnames — Edisbury, ap Howel or Powell, Kenrick, Dunbabin, would later become very familiar.

The surveyors remarked that there were in the area no mines of coal or lead, but only a small stone quarry, no common lands or waste. 'This manor, being a member of the lordship of Bromfield, doth serve at the leete and laudaies of ye said lordshipp, as they are bound to doe.' There were 17 manors in the lordship, and Marchwiel and Sonlli were part of the manor of Rhiwabon. It is noticeable that there was still not much penetration of English surnames, whilst among the Welsh, between one fifth and one third of the inhabitants retained the *ap* or *vch* (son or daughter), indicating probably monoglot Welsh speakers.

Unfortunately, this is all we know of ordinary village life until the seventeenth century, when the Vestry Books give us more details. One thing is worth noting, however; at the Battle of Bosworth in 1485, Sir William Stanley, beginning the day on the side of Richard III, decided to change his allegiance and throw in his lot with Henry Tudor — the likely winner. Sir William was at that time Lord of Bromfield and Yale, so it is just possible that there were Marchwiel or Sontley men in his personal following on the battlefield, since they would have been obliged to provide their quota on demand. In 1495, however, Sir William was accused of high treason and beheaded, and as was the usual custom, his lands were forfeit to the Crown, Marchwiel and Sontley amongst them.

3: Life in the Parish, 1660–1894

Marchwiel is fortunate in having much of its day-to-day history recorded in detail from the late seventeenth century onwards in its Vestry Books, which despite their title did not confine themselves to ecclesiastical matters. For centuries until local government was reformed in the Victorian period, the vestry and its principal officers, the churchwardens, had a dual function, both ecclesiastical and civil; their civil duties included the care of the poor, the upkeep of the roads and the keeping of the peace in general; in addition to the two wardens, annual meetings appointed overseers of the poor, surveyors of the highways and parish constables. It was necessary to post one copy of the meeting notice on the church door, and send another to the magistrates. From 1674 onwards (with an unfortunate gap from 1777 until 1800) we find, jumbled together in the same volume as is not uncommon in a small parish, the accounts of the churchwardens, overseers of the poor and surveyors of the highways, alongside details of payments for the destruction of vermin. Another feature of the accounts is the 'Brief', or royal mandate to hold a collection for some deserving cause. The document was read from the pulpit during the service and at the close, the clerk stood at the door to receive contributions, which were in turn handed to a travelling collector. In Marchwiel many such collections were made:

1679 by virtue of a noat from our Bishop for a collection for the poor of Bohemia
1s
1708 to Lisburn in Ireland 4s 1d
1709 Shadwell, Middlesex 1s 2d
1709 or ye Relief of ye poor Palatines   20s 6d

One of the earliest references in the Vestry Book is to a collection for maimed soldiers, which amounted to 16s 3d, and in 1692 there was 'collected in ye Parish of Marchwiell towards ye redemption of captives ye sum of 7s 3d'. This often referred to those captured by pirates, especially off the Barbary coast, and the collections for towns elsewhere in Britain were probably the result of disasters such as fire and flood — 4s 7d was collected for the city of York in 1695.

There is little doubt that parishioners found these dues quite a burden, especially when added to tithes, but mostly they paid up, although their willingness was severely tested by the obligation to contribute to the repair of the church and churchyard:

1674 Assessment imposed upon the people of Marchwiel (and Sontley) for and towards the repair of the church and steeple and for other necessaries thereunto belonging:-

Lady Broughton	£1 5s 0d
for her 2 tenements in Coed Dafydd	3s 6d
Coll: (Robert?) Broughton	10s 0d
Widow Edisbury	9s 9d
James ap Edward	3s 0d
Widow Dunbabin	1s 3d
John Edisbury Esq	0s 9d
Catherine Sontley	1s 6d
Mr Langley	4s 6d

A total of £9 19s 0d was raised on this occasion, whilst expenditure on repairs and maintenance in the 1660s and 1670s included the following:-

for a load of lime and for whitening of the Church to Henry of the Green 3s 9d
for mending the church wall £2 5s
lock for ye churchyard gate 7d
bread and wine at Easter 9s 0d
cutting nettles 4d; slating 2s 6d
grease for ye bells 9d
ink 1d.

In 1664 and later we read of the treasurer's perennial nightmare — 'more disbursed than received — 11s 0d'.

In 1674 householders were also assessed to contribute to the maimed soldiers' list, and again Lady Broughton headed the 1st at 7s 0d, Coll: Broughton at 2s 0d, Catherine Sontley at 4d, Mr Hanmer (the Rector) for his tenement in Pentre Meilyn 7d and Dame Broughton 1d; the old lady had apparently refused to pay the 4d required of her two years previously, but whether action was taken we are not told. In 1685 Lady Broughton was assessed at £5 6s, Catherine Sontley at 6s and Joshua Edisbury at 3s. Mr Edisbury was by now the owner of Erddig, but was only assessed for the proportion of the estate which lay within the parish. In Sontley, Mr Langley had now become Sir Francis Langley Kt, assessed at £6.

The Poor

Poor relief was administered, after the 1601 Poor Law, to those unable to maintain themselves— the old, the sick, widows, the abandoned family and illegitimate (or 'base') children. Traditionally the Poor Law has the reputation of having encouraged a self-righteous and hardfaced attitude to society's inadequates, but we should of course remember that there were no sources of funds except the rate imposed upon the more prosperous parishioners, who naturally had an interest in keeping spending to a minimum. The village was certainly a compact and self-sufficient little unit — in 1666 the is a list of names of 'all foreigners that have not paid their assessments, and others of ye parish'.

There are long lists of amounts paid out — 1715 to Ann Ralph in her sickness, 8s 6d; for her coffin and burial 6s 6d. Usually the house rent of widows was paid by the parish. Residence was the qualifying factor, and in 1721, after the list of poor to receive help, 'it is ordered that the persons overwritten wear badges'. Indeed in 1759 there is a laconic footnote by the churchwarden/overseer — 'No badge, no relief'! The badge distinguished the 'deserving poor' (sometimes referred to as 'badgers') from the assorted rogues and vagabonds, especially those from other areas, who sought to take advantage of the system. To be fair, Marchwiel seems to have had some generous overseers, who in 1729 gave 'to the woman from Chester 5s' and 'to the girl from Worthenbury 10s'. Two cottages had been built in 1727, of which one was for Simon ap Hugh and his family, near the church, 'towards which his mother gave £3 and the parish £6 8s 5d, and Dr Ffoulkes gave straw to thatch both houses'. In the following year, by the will of Lady Dorothy Jeffreys, who owned property in the parish and was the niece by marriage of the notorious Judge Jeffreys, £20 was invested which, with the interest, was to be used for the relief of the 'most necessitous poor of the parish, exclusive of such as shall be or are upon the Parish Books'. The parish added £5 17s 4d to the bequest, making it up to £40, with which the overseers 'bought therewith a House and Croft in Brymbo', and the rents from this were used for many years to relieve the poor. In 1776 the tenant was paying £2 5s 9d for the year, but the house was sold early in the nineteenth century to make bricks etc for the enlarging of Gibraltar Cottages, which had been built for the poor by subscription a hundred years earlier and named in honour of Britain's acquisition, captured from Spain in 1704. In 1746 Tristram Davenport, yeoman, took a mortgage on Gegin Wen, Minera, and five years later, by agreement with the original owners, David and Martha Davies and with the Rector, Mr Anwyl and the churchwardens, borrowed £30 on the property, to be used for the poor of Marchwiel.

The death rate among those poor was notoriously high, and paupers were buried at parish expense, but 'drink for ye ringers' was a regular and necessary allowance, as with Margaret Ralph in 1729: 'for drink for the burying of her child, 01s 01d'. There are frequent references to one Robert ap Richard, who seems to have been either 'tended' or 'fetched home' by the parish over a number of years, and in 1733 we have a list of those who contributed to the poor rate, which was at that time 3d in the pound. In 1776, £25 9s 6d was spent on the building of two more houses to be used by the poor at a small reserve rent, the Rector being responsible for them. Also in 1776 it was ordered 'that all children of such poor as receive relief from the parish shall be put as apprentices as they respectively attain the legal age — and all parish officers not putting this order into execution shall be prosecuted at the expense of the parish'. Below is a later note by some meticulous rector or clerk — 'You should have told us what age the legal one is'! In the same year there is an outright payment of £1 10s 0d 'to Clarke's children after he ran away'; if the young Clarkes survived their difficult childhood they may well have benefited from the apprenticeship arrangements. The question of extravagance was taken very seriously: in 1750 it was agreed 'that the overseers of the poor are not to exceed on account of the burying of any poor person: For ale, 1s 6d; for coffin, 5s; for a shroud, 3s'. In 1730 we read a comprehensive list of the names of the wardens and overseers 'since they were annexed'; the first pair to serve in a dual capacity were John Griffiths and Robert Eyton. On Easter Monday 1714 these two were chosen churchwardens and overseers of the poor 'for ye year ensuing ... and in consideration that they undertook both offices together, especially John Griffiths having been lately warden before, it is agreed neither of them be warden or overseer any more' (Humphrey Ffoulkes, Rector).

The duties of the churchwardens were clearly burdensome, involving not only the care of the church fabric but also a mass of paperwork — the submission of copies of the register entries (births, marriages and deaths) to the diocesan registry; they also had to attend the Bishop's and Archdeacon's courts when summoned. In 1670 we read 'Spent in appearing at the Quarter Sessions in Chester', presumably to give evidence when part of the church plate was stolen. The wardens had wide powers over the religious life of the village, since they could enforce church attendance; their social status varied, but usually they were from the farming community. Their writing is usually rather poor — indeed some could only make their mark - and the name Marchwiel is spelt in several different ways. Only once, in 1724, is a churchwarden allowed the courtesy of the title of Mr Matthew Wright (of Stryt-yr-Hwch). The unwillingness of the man in the street to undertake these duties is a well known fact, and in 1720 Robert Ellice and William Wilkinson simply refused to act. Others were often fined for non attendance at the vestry meeting. This meeting took place very frequently at the *Red Lion Inn*, opposite the church, and in the next century, from the 1820s onwards, in the new National School off Woodhouse Lane. All the officers had to present their accounts, which were 'allowed' (or otherwise) before their successors were appointed for the next twelve months, and it is clear that the vestry virtually controlled policy, making decisions about assessments, levies and expenditure of the poor rate and the church rate, and the election of one of the churchwardens, subject only to the jurisdiction of the Bishop in the case of the churchwardens, and the magistrates in all other cases. The Rector himself chose the second warden at the Easter Vestry. The presence of Welsh and English names alongside each other is informative; in 1676 the wardens were Ralph Henshaw and Howell Hughes. Names like Thomas John ap Hugh, Thomas ap Richard, Ellis ap Edward and Hugh ap Evan, run parallel with those of Edisbury, Dunbabin, Hanmer and others. By 1719 the village was decidedly half-and-half. 'agreed that Katrin ach [*ferch*] Ellis be allowed with the 5s given her by Andrew Thomas (last year's overseer) a load of coal or 5s to buy it. That Sion Cadwaladr be allowed 2s 6d per quarter this year + a load of coal'. In the vestry of 1726 it was agreed that English and Welsh should be spoken, 'that all the inhabitants might be acquainted therewith', and in 1711 a Welsh *Book of Common Prayer* was bought for 10s 6d, while John Meller of Erddig kept among his papers a receipt for 100 Welsh Bibles which he had bought for the church. It would appear, however, that for the rest of the century and into the next one English gained rapidly as the dominant language of the village. In the report to the Diocese in 1729 we see that in Dr Ffoulkes' time a service and sermon in Welsh are given once a month, the Rector stating that 'it was once a fortnight 18 years ago when I came here first', whilst in the Rural Dean's report of 1749 we are told that 'the language in church is all English excepting the second lesson, which is always in Welsh and Welsh prayers and sermon on the last Sunday morning in every month, which I believe to be a proper proportion of the two languages to be used in this church'. In 1791 the return stated that 'the service is altogether in English and has been so upwards of 16 years, since 1775 (since the death of Mr Anwyl) ... The alteration was made by desire of the parishioners in general who understand and speak English only, at least better than they do Welsh'. A century later, by the time of the 1881 Census, only about two dozen residents stated that they used both languages.

The second vestry book takes us from 1800 to 1837, a particularly difficult and troubled time throughout Britain. The country had been at war with France since 1794, and by 1801 Napoleon Bonaparte seemed destined to become master of Europe. His blockade of continental ports cut off imports, and the rise in prices soon outstripped wages; needless to say, it was the poor who suffered most. In addition, the summer of 1800 was very wet and the ruined harvests caused widespread starvation. Wheat prices had gone up from 45 shillings to 134 shillings per quarter, and by 1801 the sixpenny (2p) loaf was costing 1s 5d (7p). It is estimated that one sixth of the entire population was on poor relief or some other form of charity at this time. As a substitute staple food, rice was imported and bought in to replace bread in many places, including Marchwiel.

> *29th January 1801* — We, Henry Newcome and Samuel Strong Clerks, two of His Majesty's Justices of the Peace acting for the District of Wrexham in the County of Denbigh, at a Privy Sessions held this day do hereby order the overseers of the parish of Marchwiel in the said district, to purchase one hundred pounds of rice for the poor of the sd. parish who receive relief from the parish, to be distributed weekly, together with salted herrings in the proportion of one third of their weekly pay, and to continue doing the same 'till further notice.

Probably it is best to let the rest of the records speak for themselves. The overseers met monthly, at 'Widdow Jones's House' (*The Red Lion*) and in 1800 Elizabeth Thelwell had been allowed 2 shillings towards a pair of clogs, while a month later Elinor Jones was allowed '2 shillings towards buying a pair of Cloggs, also 3 shillings more towards buying a petticoat'.

> *1802* That Widow Jones' Fidler be allowed one grey flannel bedgown, a petticoat and one shift. In 1807 the *Red Lion's* regular musician was allowed another shift and later on '2s per week until further orders'. Clearly her tips were not generous!
>
> *1806* Christian James and Elizabeth Williams be allowed 7 shillings each for attending Jane Jones when she cut her throat — three weeks.
> Elizabeth daughter of Mary Clark be bound an apprentice to Saml. Clerk of Liverpool, shoe maker, Liner and Binder, for the term of 5 years, and that the sum of £5 be paid in hand with the said apprentice and also thirty shillings for cloathing the said girl.
>
> *1810* Occasional relief paid to a strange woman and 2 children in Distress, ill on the road, 14s.
>
> *1815* Thomas Williams, collier, being burnt in the damp (a methane gas explosion), be allowed relief on occasions as necessity requires.
> Sarah daughter of Thomas Williams (one arm) — clogs and 2 *brats* (aprons)
> James Jones, son of Molly the maid, sent to Martha Roberts.
> Anne Hughes's girl, Elizabeth, be put out to 2 years' apprenticeship as a mantuamaker at Bryn, Llangollen.
>
> *1823* Edward Jones being ill be allowed one shilling and six pence in relief and allowed four shillings further to convey him to Chester Infirmary.
> Edward Jones (*Cymro*) at present in the Infirmary be allowed a pair of flannel drawers.
>
> *1824* Sam: Stocker to convey Edward Jones (being lame) to Holywell to bathe (at

St Winifred's Well), to be allowed 20s for his journey for taking him there, and 6s per day for each day afterwards he is absent from home.

1825 The overseer to summon a family from Stryt Issa, Rhos, before the magistrates for obtaining money from the overseers fraudulently.

1826 That the fathers of all the base children on the books (if to be found) be called upon for the whole of the arrears immediately. If not paid before 29th June the Officers to apply for warrants against them.

This pursuit of errant fathers was unfortunately matched in 1818 by a decidedly savage injunction against the mothers:

That every woman being pregnant that becometh troublesome to the parish shall be imprisoned for the 1st child being born a bastard, not less than 3 calendar months, for the 2nd child ... shall be imprisoned not less than 6 calendar months and for the 3rd child: not less than 12 calendar months.

The help given to the children themselves was always practical, if lacking in warmth.

1829 Thos Williams, illegitimate child of Grace Williams, be sent round the different farmers in the Township of Sontley and parish of Marchwiel and to remain at each place for a fortnight and should any farmer wish to keep him for 12 months, the parish to clothe him when he first goes to his place and each farmer to keep him with necessary washing during each fortnight.

1831 That Mr John Roberts be allowed a new apron, a new pair of shoes a pair of stays and a new Bonnet for his servant Hannah Vaughan, base child of John Vaughan. (The signatures below include that of John Vaughan - overseer).

1835 [the list of Bastardy Payments refers to 14 children, all of whose fathers are named and presumably made some contribution. The mothers received 1s 6d per week or £3 18s per annum, and the total outlay for the parish was £52 12s 2d.]

1832 That Maria Williams be allowed a donkey and 7s per week to be stopped out of her pay until the price of the donkey runs up.

1833 That Thos Williams (one arm) take his donkey waggon to the overseers that they may judge what repair may be wanting and order the same. (John Cheetham, Vestry Clerk)

1835 That Robert Jones his wife be allowed 1s 6d per week for the keep of her child as her husband being transported.

This second volume, like the first, has the records of the poor interspersed with plans for spending on the church and also the vermin payments. In 1566 an act had been passed for the destruction of 'Noyfull Fowles and Vermin', especially crows, rooks and choughs, and its practical application fell to the churchwardens. Again and again we find references to foxes and hedgehogs in the eighteenth century records, but by the nineteenth there seems to be more interest in small birds, because of the damage which they did to crops:

1826 6d per dozen (from the church rate) paid for the heads of all rooks and crows and 3d per dozen for all other small birds. There is a request to 'gentlemen with rookeries' to decrease their numbers, 'it being so injurious to the agricultural interest of the neighbourhood', but we are not told whether the appeal succeeded.

1830 3d per dozen upon all Birds' Heads (Robbins, Rens and Swallows excepted). Hedgehogs to be paid for at 2d each.

As mentioned in an earlier chapter, the church was enlarged to its present shape in the 1820s, and in 1821 the new overseers were authorised to consult with Mr Yorke and the Commissioners of the Overton Turnpike Road regarding the proposed new wall and railings to the front of the churchyard. We have already heard what one farmer thought of all this expense! Less controversial perhaps was the health service operated by the overseers. In 1822 the vestry proposed to employ Mr Thomas Randles of Pumrhyd, Surgeon, 'to supply Physic, ointments, salves and attendance (except in case of broken or fractured bones and necessary journeys to be paid for extra) for such of the paupers as may be sick or lame and recommended by a Ticket signed by one of the Churchwardens; and to allow him a salary of four guineas per annum and the said Mr Thos Randles agrees to the above conditions ...'

Constant complaints throughout the country about the ever increasing Poor Rate led to the Whig government's decision by the Act of 1834 to replace the existing parish system with workhouses serving Unions of many parishes; the Wrexham Union, formed at a meeting at the *Wynnstay Arms Hotel* on 31st March 1837, was made up of 56 parishes and a total population of 35,000 people. Marchwiel was stated to have 499 residents, and one of the first Guardians of the Wrexham Workhouse was the Rector, Mr Luxmoore, followed by Richard Birch of Old Hall and Thomas Davies of Old Sontley. The village was none too happy about joining with the urban and mining areas around Wrexham, but its petition in 1836 to join Bangor and other rural parishes was turned down. The new system meant no more regular or occasional money payments to the parish paupers from the Poor Rate, although it was decided to continue to support the Overton Dispensary (whose services had taken over from Mr Randles) at the rate of £4 per annum. Unfortunately this was discontinued in 1838. The vestry meeting of 25th March 1837 was the last at which the parish was permitted to vote away money for the relief of its own poor, and from then on the churchwardens' and overseers' accounts were completely separate. Any help which was now given was derived from Marchwiel's own charities, which will be described later. The first two quarterly accounts of the overseers for 1837 tell their own story.

1st quarter	To the poor	£33 11s 4d
	to the Union	£46 3s 4d
	County rate	£14 13s 4d

In the second quarter, Union and County payments remained the same, but there were no more to the individual poor. Indeed, the minutes record that 'poor rates in Marchwiel having been larger in proportion to the population that in any other parish in the new Wrexham Union, the Guardians be requested to call the attention of the Board to this fact'. Some idea of the amounts involved is contained in a list drawn up in 1837 in Mr Luxmoore's hand, entitled 'Estimate & Valuation of the Landed Property in the Parish of Markwiel Made in Pursuance of an Act passed 19th of August 1836'. From it we learn that the largest property was New Sontley, owned by Simon Yorke Esq and leased to Mrs Mary Wainwright. It was assessed as being worth £328 10s 0d, and with the Poor Rate at 4d in the pound, she had to find £5 9s 8d towards relief. The *Red Lion,* owned by the Yorkes and occupied by Thomas Hughes, was assessed at £7 10s 0d and the Poor Rate payment was half a crown (12$\frac{1}{2}$p), whilst at the other end of the scale Charles Prince, who occupied glebe land of one acre, had to find only 8d. A further list mentions all the cottages, in other words every other property in Marchwiel parish, but as they are described only as "house and garden" we cannot locate them as easily as we can the farms. Their total assessment value was £123 2s 3d and this realised £2 0s 10 d. The total sum realised from the farmers, by contrast, was £65 11s 6d.

In 1838 Gibraltar was sold and seems to have realised a net sum of £103. It was described in Mr Luxmoore's hand as 'five dwellings of brick partly slated, partly thatched and the garden and yard thereunto attached, being together one eighth of an acre or thereabouts, commonly known by the name of Gibraltar. It was also unanimously agreed that it was advisable to apply the proceeds of the sale, after deducting the expense thereof, in the following manner, to the permanent advantage of the parish viz. £40 to the objects mentioned in the will of the Lady D Jeffreys (proven in the year 1728) — that sum having been wrongfully applied to the enlarging of the forenamed tenement for the use of parish paupers — & the remainder as a contribution to the Union workhouse'. A note added in 1844 says that the whole sum was afterwards applied to defraying part of the expenses of the Union House.

There is inside this book a paper dated Epiphany 1841, again written by Mr Luxmoore, noting that 'The Rector and Churchwardens of Marchwiel propose on every Sunday after evening prayer except on the first Sunday in each month, distributing bread to the poor and needy among them in the parish'. Also signed by the churchwardens, Edward Jones and Thomas Hughes.

It was also resolved that quarterly meetings be held at the National School, that the wishes of the ratepayers may be conveyed by the Guardian to the Union Board. Also that the 'Overseers return to the Guardian a revised list of all the paupers receiving parish pay and their ages and residences.' This list duly appeared and gives us a most detailed picture of the 54 people described as 'the poorer' in the village, who made up just over one tenth of the population. This list, drawn up in 1841, gives us a picture of the humbler addresses in the village, to add to the now familiar details of landlords and tenants. It included Elias Jones of the National School, who in 1843 became, in addition to his teaching duties, Vestry Clerk, with an annual salary of 30 shillings. This office he still held in 1861. Some of the locations mentioned are lost to us now — Sarah Evans of Birdsnest had 5 children, as did Ann Borras of Bank Cottage, while Maria Edwards of Pwll Sarn, near Plas Noble, had 4 children. Edward Hughes of Marchwiel Gate and Mary Hayter of Cock Bank Gate probably drew a small income from the tollgates at each end of the village, of which more will be said later. Probably the oldest resident at this time was Widow Vaughan, aged 90. Three neighbours in Gibraltar and four in Pentrellwygedd (on the bend of Bryn-y-grog Hill) also appear on the list, while the Barracks near Stryt-yr-hwch are mentioned without comment.

One name of this period deserves special attention. In April 1844 Thomas Downes aged 28, who occupied one of the glebe cottages, was found drowned in the river Dee in the Handbridge area of Chester, having spent an evening visiting several local taverns with his brother-in-law. A tragic accident whilst inebriated would not have been very surprising, but he was also found to have severe head injuries and the knees of his trousers were torn and carried traces of gravel, indicating that he had been dragged some distance. The coroner issued a verdict of 'Found suffocated and drowned', but Mr Luxmoore was very unhappy about this, being concerned for one of his own tenants, along with other Marchwiel people who were convinced that he had been killed, for whatever reason, and thrown into the river. Furthermore the inquest jury included eight publicans among its twelve members — hardly a fair balance. There was a strong feeling in the village that the police were more interested in protecting the property of the rich rather than the persons of the poor, as the Rector wrote in one of several letters to a Chester newspaper. He eventually persuaded the Home Secretary that there were sufficient grounds for believing that a murder had been committed, and a reward of £100 was offered for evidence, but it appears that none was forthcoming and the matter was dropped. Downes was buried in the churchyard a few days after his death.

In addition to the names on this list, there were a further 25 people who were 'not living in the parish but connected therewith by working therein regularly or having children in the school'. All these would have taken part in the celebrations at, for instance, the 21st birthday of Sir Watkin Williams Wynn in May 1841, when the overseers resolved to give ale and meat out on the day, — recommending that 'no band or music accompany the meat to Marchwiel (it was to be at the *Red Lion* by 11 am) and that the meat given away be mutton only, as being more convenient to divide into small portions and less waste made'. Likewise in 1846 when Mr Simon Yorke (III) married Miss Victoria Cust, well over 100 of the poor received mutton, bread and ale to mark the occasion.

In the same year, seven people were nominated to serve as overseers: Mrs Edgworth of Bryn-y-grog, Mary Owens of Pentre Meilyn, Mary Wainwright of

New Sontley, Mary Davies of Clay Farm, Chas. Edwards of the Lodge, William Morris of Cock Bank and William Roberts of Middle Sontley, and two were elected. From this time until the workhouse system came to an end almost a century later, the Poor Rate was paid directly to the Wrexham Union.

In 1846 also we have a list of those nominated to serve as parish constables — an office which dated from the Middle Ages, with duties including the serving of summonses, maintaining lists of freeholders/voters, raising recruits for the county militia, etc. Marchwiel must have been a law abiding and peaceful place on the whole, since we have very few references to the activities of the constables. A rating assessment of 1759 for a constable's tax upon the inhabitants of the township of Sontley raised the sum of 17s 5d with Mr Yorke having to contribute 1^{1}/₂d, Mr Annwill (the Rector) 1s 3d, Jonathan Moor 3s 6^{1}/₂d, Mr Moor for the Smithy 3^{1}/₂d and Randle Davenport 2s 10d. The 1846 list for Marchwiel nominated William Wilcock of Plas Noble, Wm. Pritchard of The Oak, Thos. Wilkinson of Bryn Dedwyn, John Morris of the Groves, Edward Thomas of Bryn Newydd, Meredith Evans of the Cottage, Thomas Hughes of the [*Red*] *Lion Inn* and Edward Jones of Woodhouse.

The Highways

By the Highway Act of 1555 the vestry was obliged to hold a meeting annually in September, in order to appoint 'waywardens' and levy Highway rates and we read that in Marchwiel in 1714 'at a vestry held on Whitsun Monday it was ordered for ye Highway that there be a levy of 6d in the pound for this year, and no insisting on ye six days' work of ye teams, but everyone to be paid for their teams, every day labourer to work 2 whole days' (signed Hunphrey Ffoulkes, Rector).

The first written reference to individual Surveyors appeared in 1709, when John Bettley and Robert Clark were appointed, while in 1710 the rules were firmly stated: the teams were not to be obliged to work but for wages; 'ye labourers, not being landholders, to work 3 intire days'. In 1723 sanctions were mentioned — 'every team that does not work its six days from 6 in the morn till 2 in the afternoon to pay 2s 6d per diem, and every labourer that misses a day to pay 6d'. In the following year, however, the levy was not raised 'because of the badness of the weather'; constant heavy rain would of course make both repair and use of the roads not only uncomfortable but well-nigh impossible. In 1737 there was a legal problem of whose details we know nothing, except that,

> Whereas Mr Moody has commended a lawsuit in the Exchequer in the most expensive manner against the Surveyors of the Highways, and whereas the Rector has paid 50s to an Attorney and for counsel in the case, it is now ordered in a Vestry that the parish pay what is claimed by the plaintiff out of the rent of Tyddyn Daniel now in the hands of the Rector, as witness our hands

Humphrey Ffoulkes (Rector)

Thos. Holland (Clerk)

and whereas Thos. Francis has been at the whole trouble and expense in soliciting this matter the Parsish orders Ed. Vaughan his Partner to pay him 2s.

The Surveyors' accounts for the period 1810–38 are a mine of information; in 1810/11 2d in the pound was levied and the money raised was spent as follows:

	£	s	d
282 loads of gravel at 6d per load	7	1	0
Labourers 34 days at 2s per day	3	8	0
To the Surveyors of the Turnpike	2	0	0
Paid the boy to tend the gate to the gravel pit		2	4
Paid to the wheelwright		1	4

The above reference to the Turnpike shows that the main road through the village, en route between Chester and Shrewsbury, was now subject to tolls collected at tollgates; Marchwiel was to have two of these in due course, one at Croes-y-mab and the other at Cock Bank crossroads, which are detailed in the Census returns of the nineteenth century. The road was a very busy one, being on the direct route from Chester to Shrewsbury, and there is a well known photograph of the *Red Lion Inn,* taken only just before the First World War, when the licensee was Cain Ratcliffe, formerly coachman at Erddig, showing an excursion stagecoach about to leave for Chester.

To return to 1815, we find that £3 6s 6d was paid towards making the wall at the 'Pimbrit' (Pumrhyd) Brook, and in 1821 1s 6d 'to repairing a platt (the level portion in the middle of the road) betwixt Marchwiel and Sontley at Sarnbwll' (or Pwll Sarn). In 1822 those nominated to serve as Surveyors included Jane, Christian and Elizabeth Jones of Woodhouse, of whom the last named was also a churchwarden; she was again returned as Surveyor in 1825, along with John Williams, molecatcher. In 1828/29 one pound was spent on lowering the bank opposite Croes-y-mab, and at roughly the same time the Rector, Mr Luxmoore, paid half the cost of lowering a bank in the Rectory Lane. 1829 is one of the few years when there is a reference to action by the parish constable; a summons was issued against Samuel Stocker of Sontley regarding a dispute about access to the gravel hole at Berthen Gron. Administration cost one shilling, as did the constable's serving of the summons. In 1831 there is a note in pencil to say that several persons had not provided the required teams for work; they included Mr Mainwaring of Marchwiel Hall (2 days), Richard Birch of Old Hall (2 days), Jane Jones of Woodhouse (1 day) and Dan: Owens of Pentre Meilyn (1 day). There are details of the actual labouring done by Richard Roberts and William Owens in 1836/7:

Scraping the roads from Cock Bank to Stryt-yr-hwch 6 days at 1s 6d	9s	0d
Putting gravel on roads towards Marchwiel Hall 6 days at 1s 6d	9s	0d
Work done on roads towards the Rectory 6 days at 1s 6d	9s	0d

Work done on roads from Sarnbwll to Stryt-yr-hwch 6 days at 1s 6d   9s 0d

and in the following year work done on the road from the Rectory to Pentre Meilyn took two men six weeks at six days per week, whilst that between Croes-y-mab and Marchwiel Hall took two men just three weeks. The instructions concerning labour were very detailed and were always carried out to the letter; indeed it was possible to receive a summons for labouring on the wrong day! There are countless details of the costs of wheelbarrows and shovels, gravel and large stones, and one or two confrontations at the gravel pit. The ever active Mr Luxmoore was a Surveyor on more than one occasion during the 1830s, as well as being an Overseer of the Poor and as we have already seen, one of the Board of Guardians of Wrexham Workhouse after its establishment in 1837.

It was after his death, however, that Highway Boards were set up to take over all these duties in what was intended to be an efficient fashion, but the villagers were very suspicious of these Victorian 'quangos' and a petition was signed by the inhabitants of Marchwiel and Sontley in February 1863 as a result of a special Vestry to discuss the matter.

> We, the undersigned ... having heard with extreme alarm that at the last General Quarter Sessions of the Peace for the said County, ... a provisional order was made constituting the said township of Marchwiel a Highway District for the more convenient management of the Highways ... We humbly represent that we consider the Highway Act ... to be detrimental to our interests as Ratepayers, as well as oppressive in its operation. We also wish to report that the Highways in our Township are in a good state of repair ... and the amount to be paid for salaries and other Incidental Expenses thereof will operate as a heavy burden upon your parishioners ..., unnecessary and unjust.

The signatories included Richard Birch, Meredith Evans, Elizabeth Jones, John Morris and Charles Owens, all influential members of the community, with Sontley represented by Mrs Wainwright (New Sontley), Wm. Willcock (Plas Noble), Wm. Edwards (Brook Cottage), John Davies (Berthen Gron), Mrs Eliza Davies (Old Sontley) and Robert Jones (Sontley Mill).

The vestry meetings continued along much the same lines for another fifty years, with Mr Luxmoore continuing his active role in village life until his death in 1860, when he was succeeded by Rev Stephen Donne. A vestry in that year met 'for the purpose of taking into consideration the best means of establishing and securing a Permanent Salary for the School Master and School Mistress of the Parish of Marchwiel for the education of the poor children and defraying the expenses connected with the school'. This was proposed by Mr Yorke and seconded by Mr Mainwaring, and it was unanimously agreed that 'a sum not exceeding £60 per annum be applied towards the education of poor children and the apprenticing of a certain number out of the Ellis Fund'.

The Marchwiel Charities

This reference to the Fund prompts a few words on the parish charities in general, two of which are still in existence. They were itemised by Mr Luxmoore in his usual thorough manner, in a document prepared in 1836 for the benefit of the Ecclesiastical Commissioners, as follows:

1626 Sir E. Broughton of Markwiel Hall, Knight, Owen Brereton of Borras Esq, Robt. Sontley of Sontley Esq, Kenrick Edisbury of Bedwell Gent., John Kenrick of Markwiel Gent., purchased in fee from the Crown ... an house, building and 13 acres of land called Tythyn Daniel ... to receive the rents and profits and to apply the same to and for the only use, maintenance and reparation of the Parish Church of Markwiel — Contents as surveyed A.D. 1836 14 acres 22 perches. Rent £17.

1628 James ap Edward or some of his descendants gave to the Churchwardens of the parish of Markwiel for the time being, upon trust, to receive the rents and profits of 3 pieces of land containing 12 acres 2 roods 4 perches adjoining the before mentioned Tenement of Tyddyn Daniel on the South Side, to be distributed to the industrious poor of the parish, exclusive of such as are or shall be on the Poor's Book. Rent 1836 £14 5s. (In fact the beneficiaries had to have children under 14 and rent not more than 4 acres of land.)

1695 John, son of John James (*ie* ap James, so John was James' grandson) of Bedwell, left interest of £5 to be distributed to the poor of Markwiel for ever.

1699 Simon son of John James of Bedwell, 1700 Hugh Dod of Borras,1702 Frances Williams of Markwiel and 1704 John Kenrick of Sontley, all left £5 on interest for the use of the poor.

1713 Sir E Broughton of Markwiel distributed the sum of £10 left by the will of E Broughton of Hatton Garden, Middlesex, to several poor persons.

Next on the list is Lady Dorothy Jeffreys' bequest of which we have already heard, while in 1792 Lady Ann Shackerley left £20 to the parish to be distributed. In 1819 Rev Samuel Strong received from the executors of the estate of the late Dowager Lady Williams Wynn for the poor of the parish, principal and interest amounting to the sum of £39 16s.

The only charity still in existence today is the Edwards and Ellis Fund, which has as its basis the original bequest of James ap Edward, but which was greatly augmented in 1858 by the bequest of Capt. Thomas David Ellis of Eyton Villa; he was born in 1792 and was grandson of John Ellis, surgeon, of High Street Wrexham and later of Eyton (buried in Marchwiel 1791). The Captain left to the parish the sum of £5,000 which, after tax, was used to buy Consols at 3% interest, and this remains the basis of the fund. The scheme was approved by the Charity Commissioners in 1864 and the first Trustees were Rev Stephen Donne, Mr Simon Yorke, Mr Edgworth, Mr Hope of Marchwiel Hall and Mr Wilcock, churchwarden. No person was to benefit without at least three years' residence in the parish, and in his will Captain Ellis had laid down that part of the money was to be used for educational purposes and part distributed annually at Christmas 'for ever' to the 'deserving poor, the sick poor and the aged and infirm' at the Trustees' discretion. When the account book was handed over to the new Parish Council in 1894 the balance stood at £116 11s 8d. For nearly a century and a half it has been used to finance book and money prizes for children,whilst elderly residents still benefit from Capt. Ellis's generosity.

Finally we must not forget a rather unusual charity established in 1833 — the Dorcas Society, whose object was 'to provide baby linen for needy persons resident in Marchwiel, Erddig, Eyton and Abenbury. Also sufficient funds to provide clothing for the females attending the Marchwiel Sunday School, having regard in the distribution of such clothing to attendance rather than the need of the recipient'. The fund no longer exists, but may well have been the forerunner of the Clothing Club which continued for many years longer.

As Queen Victoria's reign progressed, local government was steadily reformed so that Highway Boards and Sanitary Authorities joined the Poor Law Unions in assuming many of the functions of the vestry. In 1894, with the creation of Rural District and Parish Councils, Marchwiel moved into a new era, and although in many ways personalities and village needs did not change, the vestry was from then on concerned exclusively with church affairs.

4: Marchwiel Hall and its occupants

Mention of Marchwiel Hall today, within or outside its immediate neighbourhood, will probably bring cricket into the conversation, and rightly so; the fine ground which was established by Mr Benjamin Piercy in the 1880s and developed by the McAlpine family after the First World War, has played host to many international figures who have enjoyed its peaceful rural setting and welcoming atmosphere.

It is not often realised, however, that the elegant country house which provides a backdrop to the sport is not the only one to have occupied the site. Nothing is known of the appearance of the former house, but it is believed to have been replaced in the early 19th century by the present Hall built a few yards in front of it. A stone in the wall of the stable block to the rear, dated 1693, indicates that this is a part of the original establishment. Perhaps the most distinguished family in the parish between the late sixteenth and early eighteenth centuries was that of the Broughtons of Marchwiel Hall; not only were they active in the neighbourhood, but they also played an important part in national affairs, especially at the time of the Civil War.

The family name was associated with Broughton, near Worthenbury, and also with other families of the same name in Gresford, Llay and elsewhere; the result was that even the respected historian of the Wrexham area, A N Palmer, writing in 1900, had to confess that the disentangling of all the threads was an almost impossible task. It is to his detailed account that I have referred for much of this material.

In the middle of the reign of Queen Elizabeth 1 we find an Edward Broughton living at Plas Issa (Lower Hall) in Isycoed; he is mentioned in a document of 12 November 1576 along with his brothers — Lancelot, Francis (who was at 'the University') and Valentine. The latter is probably the Alderman of Chester who in 1603 left money to support the first grammar school in Wrexham. Edward left Plas Issa to his eldest son Morgan Broughton, who was busy consolidating his estate in Marchwiel as early as 1594, when he leased 'from Jasper Mottram and Elizabeth his wife of Marghweale a messuage and appurtenances in Marghweale' for the sum of £100. Morgan Broughton was sheriff of Denbighshire in 1608, and was married, sometime before 1598, to Margaret Parry, daughter of Henry Parry Esq (also known as Henry ap Harri and Harry Parry) of Basingwerk and Marchwiel Hall. This Henry Parry was something of an opportunist who had been granted the lands of Basingwerk Abbey near Holywell in 1540, after Henry VIII's attack on the monasteries. Parry's name appears next in deeds dated 1575/6 and again in 1578 when he entered into mortgage agreements, with his wife 'Katheryn Parrye', the other parties being David ap Robert ap Hoell and Jane verch Robert, his wife. It was perhaps at this time that the first Marchwiel Hall was built or extended.

We see here the vital part played by a useful marriage in the consolidation of an estate; Margaret Parry's mother Katherine was one of the Flintshire Mostyns and had been married first to William Dymock of Penley, then to Henry Parry, who was twice Sheriff of Flintshire, and thirdly (after Parry's death before 1590) to Richard Leighton, who was stated in 1620 to hold Marchwiel Hall and more land in the parish than anyone else. In this way, this much-married lady and her daughter had between them united five families, at least in law and in landed interest. Both Henry Parry and Richard Leighton were buried in the old church in Marchwiel. Richard and Katherine Leighton were commemorated, following their deaths in 1622 and 1623, on a memorial placed 'Against ye south wall of ye chancell within a pew lately belonging to ye Broughtons'.

Extract from the will of 'Henry Parrey Esq of Marchwiell', 12 Sept. 1589:

I will my body to be buried in the parish church of Marchwiell. I bequeath the sum of 40s to be employed and divided among the poorest sort of people dwelling in the parish ... I bequeath to my son-in-law Morgan Broughton Esq and Margaret his wife my daughter, my best gelding with saddle and bridle ... all the lands ... which I have in the realm of England and Wales to my son Thomas Parry and to his heirs lawfully begotten ... and in default of such issue to my daughter Margaret Broughton and her lawful heirs ...

Overseers (executors) included Thomas Mostyn and Parry's brother Bennet ap Thomas ap Harry of Perth y Maen, Flintshire. Thomas Parry did apparently die without issue and Henry Parry's estate in Marchwiel therefore went to his daughter, Margaret Broughton, although in practice not until after her mother's and Leighton's death. (It appears that Mr Leighton was a literary connoisseur and a patron of Welsh poetry in particular.)

Extract from the will of John Mostyn (brother of Katherine Broughton), March 1609/10:

> to Edward Broughton, son and heir of Morgan Broughton Esq, the lands sometime in tenure of dauid ap John ap Jenkyn 'in leangth from the Lande called Kae'r scubor (the Barn field) on th' one ende and the lande called Kae rhwng y ddwyffordd (the field between the two roads)in the other end, and in bredth between the Lande called yr Acre yslaw y ffordd (below the road) on the one side and the heighwaye that leadeth from Bangor to the Pumrhydd', 'being coppehould (copyhold) landes'.

This bequest refers to Morgan Broughton's son and heir, who was to become the first Sir Edward, knighted at Hampton Court Palace in 1617/8, and it is clear that the family's activities now took on a wider aspect; in fact the 17th century Broughtons probably spent as much time in London as they did in Marchwiel. Edward married Frances Tyrrell, who was sufficiently well connected to become a lady-in-waiting to King James I's daughter Princess Elizabeth, who married the German Elector Frederick and later, with him, assumed the throne of Bohemia. The two ladies corresponded, and it appears that the Queen sent Frances portraits of herself and the Elector, with lead busts of her sons, Rupert and Maurice, whom she described as 'fine boyes'. These mementoes were kept at Marchwiel Hall for over a century, but later disposed of.

The first Sir Edward spent the years up to the outbreak of the Civil War consolidating his property in the area, both freehold and leasehold; Norden's Survey of 1620 lists him as 'Edwardus Broughton miles (soldier) holding Maesyllan', in Marchwiel. In 1642, however, the whole country was plunged into bitter conflict, and the consequences affected the Marchwiel Hall family as deeply as any, although as far as we know no Broughton lost his life in the fighting. Sir Edward naturally took the side of the King, as did his two brothers, Captain William Broughton of Bersham and Colonel Robert, who lived at Stryt-yr-hwch; his three sons were also deeply involved, but here we note the real tragedy of civil war — the two older ones, Lieutenant Edward and Major Robert, fought for the King but the third son, Francis, was a captain in the army of Parliament in his early twenties.

A few weeks after the king raised his standard in Nottingham and began the war officially, Denbighshire and Flintshire were raising a regiment of foot to join him,

Ralph Broughton of Plas Issa, Isycoed

Edward = Eleanor Dymock   Lancelot   Valentine   Francis   Henry Parry   = Katherine Dymock (née Mostyn)
(Died 1617)   (Died 1625)   (Died 1576)   (Died 1603)   of Marchwiel & Basingwerk   She later married Richard
                                                                  (Died before 1589/90)   Leighton of Marchwiel

Morgan   = Margaret
(1544-1614)   (Living 1660)
HSD 1608

Sir Edward   =   Frances Tyrrell   Thomas   William   Robert of Stryt-y-hwch
Knighted 1617/8   Lady in Waiting to Elizabeth,   Captain Royalist Army   Colonel Royalist Army
(Died before 1660)   later Queen of Bohemia

Sir Edward = 1. Alice Honywood
              2. Mary Wyke (née Knightley) = Aquila Wyke   Francis, Captain in Parliamentary Army 1648   Robert, Major Royalist Army 1646
Captured at Chirk, 1659   Keeper of Gatehouse Prison, Westminster
Fatally wounded in naval
battle 1665. Buried in   Edward   Aquila
Westminster Abbey   Died Wrexham 1703

Edward   Aquila of Marchwiel &   Martha = Stephen Browne   Mary = William Rockwood
Born 1660/61   Llwyn Egryn   Died 1778
HSD 1698   HSD 1743   Buried Marchwiel
Died 1718   Buried Marchwiel 1772
Buried Marchwiel
                              Lucy Lewis 2 =   Charles of Marchwiel &   = 1. Anne Rockwood
                              Sold Marchwiel Hall 1801   Llwyn Egryn   Buried Marchwiel 1785
                              to Samuel Riley of Pickhill HSD 1789, HSF 1790
                                                           Died 1795

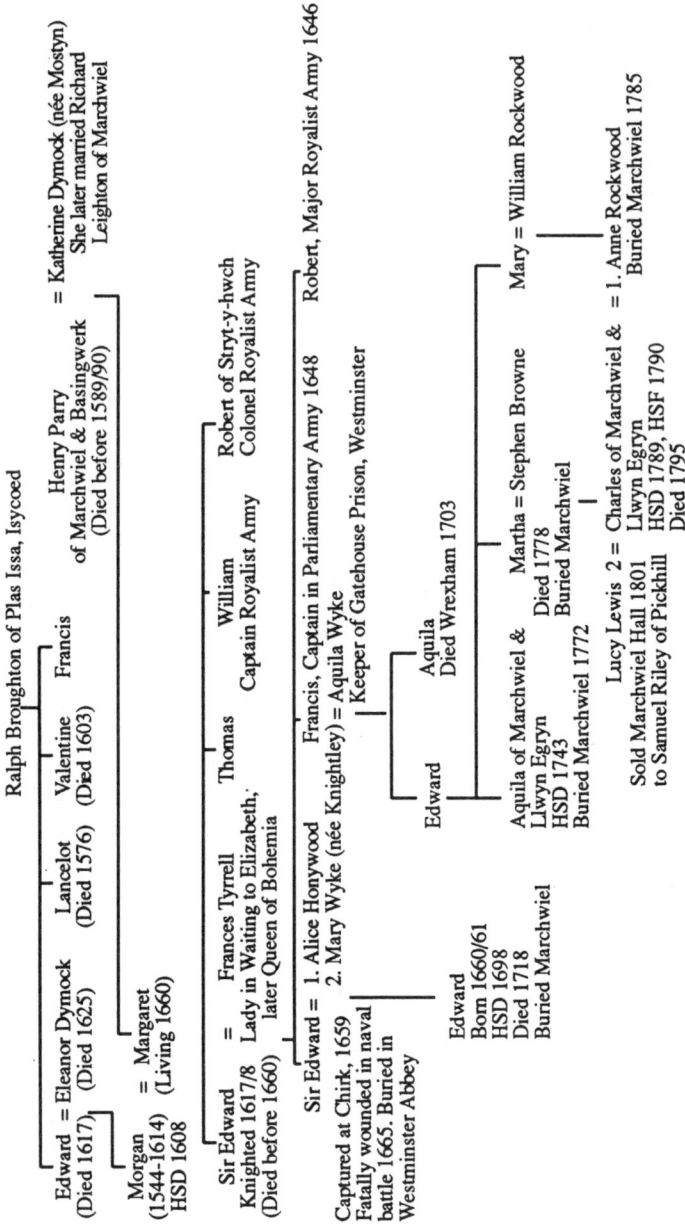

Broughtons of Marchwiel

and Lord Strange, Denbighshire's Lieutenant, appointed as Sir Edward one of the Commissioners to receive the money which was being collected, over £1,000 being needed. Sir Edward was already experienced in handling the county's fundraising during Charles' period of governing without Parliament in the 1630s, and his brother William had already raised and officered a company of men for whom he had to provide £100 as 'coat and conduct' money; this small group did good service for the King in North Wales and on the Welsh border. This same William had been one of the churchwardens in Wrexham in 1637 and after the restoration of the monarchy in 1660 he seems to have lived for a time at the Hall.

The Parliamentary commander in North Wales was Sir Thomas Myddelton of Chirk (1586–1666) who was also MP for Denbighshire and had opposed the king in the parliamentary debates which preceded the outbreak of war. However, before hostilities he had undoubtedly been on friendly terms withthe Broughtons. Lady Frances had a sister, Hester, who married Sir Thomas Salusbury of Llewenni, and when their child was born in 1634, there was a receiving ceremony in Bodfari Church after his private baptism; the two godfathers were Sir Thomas Myddelton and Sir Roger Mostyn, and also present were Sir Edward Broughton and his wife — who was of course the baby's aunt. Despite these family links, we find that nine years later Myddelton had garrisoned the town of Wem and in the two days of fighting which followed, Major Robert Broughton was wounded; he was, however, one of the lucky ones — we are told that six carriages full of bodies left the field. It appears that the young Edward, later to succeed his father to the estates, was also wounded at Wem and returned to his home. What followed leads us to guess that perhaps both of them were at home in Marchwiel Hall recovering when the Parliamentary forces marched through Nantwich and Holt, took Wrexham and seemed to be triumphant; in October 1643 Sir Edward and his two sons were 'fetched' (*ie* taken by force) from under their own roof and imprisoned in Nantwich on the orders of Myddelton, who in June had been appointed by Parliament to the unusual military rank of Sergeant Major General in North Wales. One can almost hear the sound of hooves and harness as Myddelton's troop rode down Marchwiel Hall Lane in search of their opponents. The family could not have been held in Nantwich for very long, for in the following year Edward was serving Prince Rupert at Newark and later probably took part in the disastrous battle of Rowton Moor, which was watched by King Charles himself from the walls of Chester, although the Wrexham area had by now been retaken by the Royalists.

Also active in the service of Prince Rupert was Edward's uncle, Colonel Robert, who had fought overseas in the 1630s. At the outbreak of the Irish Rebellion in 1641 he took 1000 Denbighshire men to Ireland, where they served between 1641 and 1643. Rupert, as well as being the King's nephew, was President of the Council of Wales, and the Colonel accompanied him from the Welsh border to Newark and back. Clearly he was highly thought of by Rupert, and after he had marched successfully through Lancashire, helping to capture Liverpool and relieve York, he was made Governor of Shrewsbury on his return. In this capacity he led his troops to relieve the Parliamentary siege of Montgomery, where he was shot and captured, although released soon afterwards. After this very active military career, in the late 1640s he seems to have settled at Stryt-yr-hwch with his wife, Mary Bagot of Blithfield, Staffs. A deed of 1666 shows that the Bagot family still had an interest in Sontley Mill, less than half a mile from Stryt-yr-hwch.

After the trial and execution of the King in 1649 we have little information on how the Broughtons fared during the Commonwealth period; one detail suggests that Lieutenant Edward was at the Battle of Worcester in 1651, when Charles II tried unsuccessfully to regain the throne, was captured and tried for treason, released on parole and went abroad for a time, at least until the death of Oliver Cromwell in 1658. We do know, however, that Colonel Robert was still living at Stryt-yr-hwch in that year, and a letter written in 1657 by one of his neighbours, Mrs Ursula Sontley of Sontley Hall to her cousin Mr Edisbury, gives a rare personal glimpse:

> Owld Mistress Broughton was praid for in our church (Marchwiel) this day and the Collonell did weepe very much. It is to be feared it will breack his hart.

I have not been able to discover whether 'Mistress Broughton' is his mother, Dame Margaret, or his wife Mary, but the letter is a very touching and personal reference to an ordinary morning service in 1657.

In 1659 the political situation again became tense and uncertain as a return of the monarchy became a distinct possibility, and a rather premature Royalist rising in Cheshire was joined by — of all people — Sir Thomas Myddelton, who had transferred his sympathies a few years earlier and now declared openly for Charles II. At least three of the Broughtons joined him and the Myddelton papers tell us that 'the sum of 10 shillings was paid to Coll. Broughton for what he laid out for intelligence'. Chester fell to their forces, Edward having returned from exile to command a regiment of foot at Winnington Bridge, but Parliament's General Lambert retook the city and pursued the Royalists to Chirk, which he besieged until lack of water forced the 150 defenders to surrender.

Among the prisoners taken to London was Captain Edward Broughton; after his capture 'it was feared he would lose his life on account of having broken a former parole' (according to the Wynn papers) but instead he spent the next few months in the Gatehouse Prison, which was situated near the West end of Westminster Abbey in the Tothill Street area. He was by now a widower in his early forties and while in custody he fell in love with the young widow of the Keeper of the Gatehouse, Aquila Wyke. Mistress Mary Wyke, the daughter of William Knightley Esq of Kingston on Thames, had been left with three children and had also inherited her husband's duties and 'perks' as Keeper; she eventually agreed to marry her temporary guest, but only subject to certain conditions. These conditions make the union between the Broughtons and the Wykes one of the most astonishing stories to be found in any family. The Lieutenant (who was soon to be released and knighted for his loyalty by a grateful Charles II) conveyed all his tenements and lands in the counties of Denbigh, Flint and Chester to William Knightley Esq, and John Mills Esq and his estate was declared to be worth £550 per annum free from incumbrance, except the life interest of Dame Frances Broughton in Plas Issa. His mother was still living, and Marchwiel Hall is mentioned as being in the tenure of Margaret Broughton, grandmother of the grantor, which leads us to conclude that his father had by now died.

The bride to be was obviously still not convinced of her betrothed's suitability as a good match, and a week later he wrote the 'Imprecation' printed in the 1810 edition of Pennant's *Tours in Wales*; even a century and a half later this document was regarded as something well out of the ordinary:

> I, Edward Broughton, for love, in ye presence of ye great God of heaven and earth … do implore the God of spirits to power down his vengeance upon mee … and that my name and person may stinck upon earth and molest ye nostrills of men … If I do not utterly forbear all rash swearing, and all manner of drinking, and all manner of debauchery whatsoever; or if ever I am guilty of finding fault with anything my intended wife shall doe or say; or if ever I undertake any business, or anything how great a concern soever, or small, without the knowledge, assent, consent, advice of Mary Weeks (or Wyke) my intended wife, and is to be Mary Broughton when this shall take effect; or if shee shall make any request unto me in her lifetime, it shall be of force never to be violated by me, although I surviving her, concerning body and soule, life or fortune, children or friends how unreasonable soever; or if there shall happen any difference betwixt her and me, as there hath been betwixt me and my first wife, then, if I am the cause of it, lett these and all plagues imaginable fall on me, and all the plagues God can inflict; or if shou'd arise any quarell, and shee the only cause, yet when I remember hereof, or shee these vows, I most heartily pass by, forgive and endeavour to pacifie and use all the art imaginable to please her, and if she could impose more, I wou'd most willingly doo it; or else may all those plagues, if there were greater curses or imprecations, I heartily pray that they may all be powered downe, as the rain fall on the thirsty ground, and upon my posterity for ever; and this I doe heartily and voluntarily, and with serious consideration and premeditation, having taken a long time to consider this; and now most readily signe itt with my owne hand and seal it with my owne seal". Edward Broughton. April 12 1660.

The pair were married in 1660 and had three sons, two of whom died in infancy; the only survivor, Edward, eventually succeeded to the Marchwiel estate under his mother's will. The Chirk papers tell us that the friendship with the Myddeltons continued — Sir Thomas's son was in London in 1661 and the steward records: 'March 11 Paid to my master to give the nurses etc. at the christening of Sir Edward Broughton's child £1 10s 0d.' In the following year also the young Sir Thomas and his family made the seven day coach journey to London from Chirk, and the steward records 'Dec. 5 Paid for 2 qts of ale for Sir Edd. and Major Broughton — 4d. Dec. 18 Paid for hay and oates for the mares when you dyned at Sir Edd. Broughton — 0 1s 0d'.

Clearly Sir Edward had now succeeded his father to the title and the Marchwiel estate, and his bride is the Lady Broughton referred to in the early entries in the parish Vestry Book beginning in 1663. She even succeeded in altering the name of their home, on paper at least, from Marchwiel Hall to 'Conqueress Hall' and it appears thus in her will (dated January 20th 1680/1); in a document of 1749 too, we find the house described as 'Marchwiel Hall alias Conqueress Hall'. The estate now comprised the Hall with the demesne lands annexed; one of two farms called Stryt-yr-hwch; one of two farms called Croes-y-mab; Coed Dafydd; one of two called Pont-y-ffrwd; Tyddyn-tu-uwch-y-llan; Tyddyn-tu-is-y-llan and other farms in Marchwiel, Pumrhyd Mill and other lands in Abenbury, Caernarvon Hall in Mount Street, Wrexham, and of course the Plas Issa property extending from Isycoed into the parish of Church Shocklach in the county of Cheshire, totalling about 706 acres in all. By the marriage Sir Edward also acquired two stepsons, Edward and Aquila Wyke. Lady Broughton was clearly a shrewd and determined woman and it has been said that this ensured that the estate was passed on intact, when her less businesslike husband might have allowed it to be dispersed.

The partnership between the second Sir Edward and Mary Wyke was to be shortlived, for in 1665 he was seriously wounded, serving under James Duke of York in a naval battle with the Dutch off Lowestoft on 3rd June 1665; he died a fortnight later at his home in the Gatehouse. Canon David Lloyd, an intensely Royalist cleric, wrote in his Memoirs, 'he valeantly lost his life, scorning to fall, though in effect killed, and in his stubborn way blundring out Commands when he could not speak them'. He is buried in Westminster Abbey 'in the North part of the cross aisle near the monument door'. Probably he had spent little or no time in Marchwiel after 1659; he had been given a share in the Wyke family's leases on the Gatehouse and Convict prisons; and his will, dated 21st October 1664, reflects this. To his son Edward Broughton he left (after Lady Mary's death) his house between the two prisons; the Gatehouse and the custody of its prisoners went to Edward Wyke and all the rest of his estate went first to his wife and then to his own son. One of the executors was his cousin Sir Timothy Tyrrell (Dame Frances' nephew and Governor of Cardiff) who received '£20 to buy a nagg for his care and pains'.

In 1670, according to the hearth tax returns, the Hall was occupied by Captain Broughton and Mrs Anne Broughton, and contained 12 hearths; possibly this refers to Francis, who had fought for Parliament, but we cannot be sure. Throughout the 1670s and up to 1685 Lady Mary Broughton's name appears at the top of the vestry's assessment list (the last time for the sum of £5 6s) but also on the list, at a different property which is not specified, is a Dame Broughton; indeed in 1672

'Madam Broughton' refused to pay her contribution of 4d for Denbighshire maimed soldiers. This is surprising when we note that the late Sir Edward was actually one of their number after all his Civil War disasters.

Meanwhile Lady Mary, in her role as Keeper of the Gatehouse prison, was accused in 1672 of extortion of excess fees and also of hard usage of the prisoners; she was fined 100 marks and removed from office. This seems to confirm the view that she was a tough, no-nonsense personality, who had no doubt found it easy to dominate her easygoing second husband. Her own will is dated 1680/1 and in it she left the whole of the Marchwiel estate, if Edward Broughton should die without lawful issue '... to Aquila Wyke and his lawful heirs'. Her 'undutifull sonnes', Edward and Aquila Wyke got only annuities of £40 each; likewise her 'unfortunate undutifull daughter Mary Decombe' received just £50, 'she having formerly imbeazled much of my estate'. Clearly this was not a lady to offend! The uncommon name Aquila appears to have caught the fancy of Marchwiel parents; Aquila Evans, son of Ellis and Abigail, was baptised on February 25th 1693, followed by Aquila Pugh, son of Simon and Elizabeth, in 1719.

Edward Lluyd's survey of the parish in 1699 stated that 'Sir Edward Broughton has a warren adjoyning to his Hall', and it is pleasing to know that this warren still exists. The third Sir Edward assumed the title of baronet and was High Sheriff of Denbighshire in 1698; we can deduce from this that his father had perhaps been offered a baronetcy just before his death but that it had not been confirmed. Certainly some documents refer to him as Kt and Bart, and this must have persuaded his son of his hereditary right to the title. The Rector of Marchwiel appears to have been convinced — Sir Edward died unmarried and was buried at Marchwiel on June 14th, 1718, and the register describes him as a baronet. So also does the surveyor commissioned by John Meller to assess the status of his new neighbours among the gentry as he prepared in about 1714 or 1715 to take over the Erddig estate; he goes on to give the only local description which we have of any of the family — 'He (Sir Edward) lives private and conserns himself in no publick affaires'. This remark is not strictly true, Sir Edward was High Sheriff in 1698 and there exists a letter from him to Sir Richard Myddelton 'at Cherke Castle' in which he writes :

> Mr Cotton, sonne to Sir Robert Cotton of Cumbermeere, is desired by several Gentlemen of this County to stand for the burrough of Denbigh in the ensueing Parliament. now pray give me leave to tell you, I know there has antiently bine a Corespondence betwixt your Anchestors and his, and I thinke they have both served togeather for this County severall times. now my request is, that you will assist him with your voate and interest, and you have but to commande.
> Sr Yr: most humble servant Edward Broughton
> Marchwiell July the 18th 1698

John Meller's survey goes on to describe the Marchwiel estate as being worth

£800 per annum. This period is a very confused one in the family's story and although deeds, wills etc. are quite clear and consistent, the actual number of Broughtons, including cousins, makes a full study impossible. Mr Morgan Broughton was buried in Marchwiel in 1699, but his relationship to Sir Edward remains unclear. The Wrexham historian A N Palmer remarked in 1900 that the family tomb of the Broughtons in Marchwiel Churchyard included an inscribed slab of shaly stone, but that the inscription had completely flaked off; if this were still in existence and legible, it would be of tremendous help and interest to us today. Sad to say, we cannot now even identify the tombstone itself with any certainty. A memorial in the old church (as well as the register of burials) declared that Edward Broughton of Hatton Garden, Middlesex was buried there in 1713 and it is likely that he was Sir Edward's half-brother

Sir Edward was succeeded in 1718 by his nephew, another Aquila Wyke, his step-brother having died in Wrexham in 1703. This Aquila signed the vestry minutes in 1721 so he was at least resident in the Hall from time to time, but he had also acquired the estate of Llwyn Egryn, Mold (now at the centre of the Shire Hall complex), and he seems to have been mortgaging and leasing out his Denbighshire properties frequently; indeed for several years in the 1730s, Marchwiel Hall was tenanted by the Rev Thomas Holland of Berw, who is described in the Vestry Book as 'clerk'. There is also a grave in the churchyard bearing the name of Tristram Davenport of Marchwiel Hall (died 1763); it seems clear that the Hall was leased to tenants for considerable periods. It was Mr Wyke's name which appeared at the head of the Assessment lists for Marchwiel in 1759 and 1760, however - he was to contribute £7 8s 3d to the county levy and 3s 10d on some lesser warrant. Surprisingly, however, the name of Tristram Davenport also appears on the second list as being required to find 2s 8d. When Aquila Wyke died in 1772, he was buried in Marchwiel and the estates of Marchwiel and Llwyn Egryn went to Mr Stephen Browne, husband of his sister Martha, passing next to his son Charles Browne, who was Sheriff of Denbighshire in 1789 and of Flintshire in 1790, the latter despite an Indenture dated 1776 indicating that Charles Browne now assigned his interest in Llwyn Egryn to Elizabeth, widow of Aquila Wyke. On Mr Charles Browne we have another interesting pen-portrait by 'Nimrod': '... An extraordinary character ... of a naturally kind disposition ... yet he was formerly known as 'Bloody Browne'...', presumably since he fought in the siege of Havana during the wars of the mid-eighteenth century. There was perhaps another reason, however; the Brownes had previously lived in London and 'Nimrod' relates the following anecdote:

> His garden (in London) had been robbed of much of its choicest fruit and he, being an old soldier, was not one to be trifled with ... He applied to a dissecting room in London and obtained the leg of a human being, fresh cut from the body, on which he put a stocking and a shoe and then suspended it in a man-trap over his garden wall. ... His fruit was afterwards safe.

The Rev Samuel Strong was one of Charles Browne's executors and described how among his papers he found reference to some correspondence with a member of the nobility. One of them read:

> Unless I receive an acknowledgment of either one or the other (of two earlier letters) in a week from this time, you will hear from me in that language which one gentleman uses towards another when he considers himself insulted.

His lordship did at last reply, pleading pressure of parliamentary duties. Mary Wyke would have been proud of her great-grandson! It appears that it was after Charles Browne's time that the leaden busts of Prince Rupert and Prince Maurice were melted down, while the portraits of their parents, the King and Queen of Bohemia were dispersed at one of the sales which now took place. Mr Browne died at Bath in 1795 having been married twice, first to Anne Rockwood and secondly to Lucy Lewis, both cousins on the Wyke side, but leaving no children to succeed him. The estate was therefore put up for sale; Lot 6, including Plas Issa and Dutton Diffaeth was sold to various purchasers including Lord Kenyon and Mr John Edgworth, but the Hall itself and its lands remained in Mrs Lucy Browne's hands until 1801 when it was bought for £7,000, along with its two pews in Marchwiel Church, by Samuel Riley Esq of Pickhill. After two centuries it had finally passed out of the family. There is no evidence for the belief (reasonable though it may have been) that Old Hall, about half a mile away down Woodhouse Lane, was the original home of the Broughtons, since the name was not used before the nineteenth century; its deeds mention fields which do not appear at all in the Broughton estate records, yet can be seen in the Old Hall papers up to the twentieth century.

The Hall in the nineteenth century

Mr Riley left the estate to Thomas Parker of Astley, Cheshire, who went on to sell it by auction in 1824; this was after he had rejected several offers which did not meet his expectations, including one of £50 per acre from Simon Yorke of Erddig. This time the purchaser was Samuel Boydell of Manor, in the parish of Hawarden. He held it for only five years and in 1831 it was bought for £11,000 by Mr Townshend Mainwaring, MP, JP, of Llyndir. There is among the Hall papers a fascinating document — Wyley's Farming Account Book for 1834, an essential reference for the gentleman farmer and his bailiff. We learn that Mr Mainwaring's butler was paid £30 per year, his housekeeper £20, the housemaid £12 and the kitchenmaid £7, and we are also given details of the weather for five months of that year: March — fine, sunny, dry. April — Very dry, hot sun, frosty nights. May - fine, though too hot and dry to be seasonable. June — Very dry. Pastures much burnt. July — very dry — rain came down copiously about the 26th.

The Mainwaring family owned the Hall at the time of the 1851 Census, which reveals that they had three children (commemorated in the chancel windows in the

Marchwiel Hall, c1910.   *[Mr John Bell]*

church) and that the house was staffed by a butler, a coachman, a housekeeper and seven other servants. Samuel P Hope Esq of Betley Hall, Staffs., bought the house from Mr Mainwaring in 1861 for the sum of £13,451 and his widow, Mrs Amelia Hope, sold it in 1882 to Benjamin Piercy Esq for £18,437.

Mr Piercy was a noted civil engineer and a native of Montgomeryshire; he worked with Henry Robertson when the latter surveyed the line from Chester to Shrewsbury and was concerned in nearly all the plans for railway development in Wales, including the bridge across the Mawddach estuary at Barmouth. Not all his plans for Wales were carried out, and perhaps his career frustrations in this country led him to be increasingly involved with railway construction in Sardinia, where he became a personal friend of Garibaldi and his family. The Piercys had a house in London also, but his active business and social life did not deter Mr Piercy from building the cricket ground at the Hall, attracting visitors and local people to his home. After his death at his London home in 1888 Mrs Piercy continued to be involved in village life and was a very good friend of the new school, which had been built in the village in 1874. She became one of the Managers and the children were regularly invited to the Hall for tea or presented with her prizes for progress. In the early years of this century her charitable fund gave at least £850 to the school, which was used for much-needed building work and classroom needs. The church also benefited from her generosity; the organ was presented in memory of Mr Piercy and after her own death in 1912 her name was perpetuated by her family with the donation of the present pulpit; the Piercy Hall in the centre of the village (opened in 1906) and also Piercy Avenue, the first post-war new housing, ensure that the family name will not be forgotten.

The McAlpine Family

The Hall and estate were again put up for sale, on 14th July 1913, and as in the past the property was offered for sale in 6 lots, of which Lot 1 was made up of the Hall and 189 acres, with the two pews in Marchwiel Church. (The auctioneer at the Wynnstay Hotel in Wrexham was Mr Frank Lloyd). In due course Mr Alfred McAlpine moved in with his wife, the former Miss Ethel Williams of Aboyne, Aberdeenshire, and their three children. They were soon settled into the life of the landed families of the neighbourhood; the family possesses a letter dated 22nd April 1920 from Mr Philip Yorke of Erthig Park (note the Yorkes' spelling of their estate name, which is probably the original):

Dear Mrs McAlpine

Will you and Mr McAlpine give us the pleasure of your company on Wednesday afternoon next at about 3 p.m., bringing any of your nice little family.

You will be meeting the Most Hon'ble Marquis and Marchioness of Cambridge, the former being as no doubt you are aware, Brother to our Queen. (Queen Mary).

With our united very kindest regards, believe me to remain ever.

Very sincerely yours
Ph Yorke

The family is very proud of its descent from the Highland Clan McAlpin, the new occupant of the Hall being one of the sons of Sir Robert McAlpine, civil engineer and founder of the construction company. A biography by J Saxon Childers, privately circulated in 1925, tells of the young Robert's capacity for hard work, common among young Scots of unprivileged background and anxious to make their way in the world. The firm was involved in the building of a new town on Clydebank in the 1890s and in major works for the Singer Company — in 1883 the main factory, in 1904 the cabinet factory and in 1906 rebuilding the japanning factory after a fire at its premises in Kilbowie, Glasgow. A man seen running to help put out the flames was assured that all was under control, but his reply says a great deal: 'I'll no' walk, for if I do, McAlpine will have rebuilt the place before I get there'!

The firm's reputation for speedy work dated from its development of the ferrolithic process; this mixture of steel furnace slag and Portland cement in the ratio of 4 parts to 1 revolutionised the construction industry. In June 1914, heavy rain demolished the railway bridge at Aviemore; there was disastrous loss of life, but McAlpines had completed the replacement by 8th July, with normal traffic being resumed a week later. The outbreak of the First World War meant increased business, and in 1917 a factory dedicated to shell filling was built in record time in

Georgetown, Glasgow and at cost only — McAlpines decided to forego their commission and profits. The letter of thanks from Whitehall was signed, on 30th June 1917, by a certain Michael Heseltine! Lord Kitchener also had occasion to thank the company for its part in the war effort, and it is not surprising that a knighthood soon followed for its head. Sir Robert married twice and had a large family; one of his daughters, Miss Roberta McAlpine, was married in 1917 at Bath Abbey to Richard Lloyd George, elder son of the Prime Minister. One of the bridesmaids was the bridegroom's sister and future MP Miss Megan Lloyd George, who a year or so later accompanied her father to the Peace Conference at Versailles.

Normal work was resumed after the war, with the building of the Dorchester Hotel in London and perhaps the best known of all McAlpines' contracts, the construction of Wembley Stadium for the Empire Exhibition of 1924. The first turf was cut by the Duke of York (later King George VI) in January 1922 and the building was completed by April 1923. For those who enjoy statistics, the circumference was equal to that of the walls of Jericho — half a mile. Three thousand trees were felled and 150,000 tons of clay were dug up and removed. The turf of the arena had come from a golf course and had been tended for nine months before its removal to Wembley.

During this whole period Sir Alfred (himself knighted in 1932) found time to take a prominent part in the social and public life of Denbighshire and of Marchwiel in particular. The cricket ground flourished and a fine pavilion was built as a memorial to Lady McAlpine's brother, Lieut. James Williams of the Lancashire Regiment, who had been killed in France in 1916. Sir Alfred was, at various times, President of Wrexham Football Club and Chairman of Wrexham Conservative Association and also owned several racehorses. From 1939 until his death he was President of Denbighshire Cricket Club. Teams visiting the Marchwiel ground in the early days, such as Rhos in 1914, must have been slightly surprised to find two delightful thatched summerhouses serving as changing rooms, with refreshments served by the butler and his staff.

In 1918, near the end of the First World War, a Grand Charity cricket match and Fete, one of several, was held at the Hall in aid of the RWF Benevolent Fund and the Wrexham Hospitals, in the course of which a leather-bound Bible signed by the Prime Minister, Mr Lloyd George, was auctioned. Twenty years later a very similar event again took place at the Hall, this time in aid of the Piercy Hall and Wrexham Hospital, and opened by Lord Derby. One wonders how many of the crowds present had any forebodings as to how close they were to another terrible conflict; in fact it was just over a year later that the country was again at war. At this time the firm of McAlpine generously arranged to construct a large air-raid shelter, lined and roofed with concrete as we might expect, in the grounds of the school, just over the fence from the School House lawn. The shelter was for the use of those living in the middle of the village; many will remember the nights spent in its depths, and even the occasional day, a particularly memorable one being an afternoon Prize Distribution at Christmas, which was interrupted by an air-raid warning. The prizes were abandoned in the school building and children, teachers and guests completed the proceedings "down below".

Sir Alfred died in 1944 and is buried in the new cemetery. His widow, who lived until 1961, lies alongside him, their resting place appropriately marked by a Celtic cross as a tribute to their Scottish ancestry. His control of the Northern and Midland section of the firm passed to his only son, Mr A J ('Jimmie') McAlpine, like his father a keen sportsman, who lived at Gerwyn Hall, just over the parish boundary. He continued Sir Alfred's interest in cricket and was an active player for many years. The Hall itself had passed to Sir Alfred's daughter and son-in-law, Mr and Mrs Peter Bell, and from 1962 onwards they continued the family tradition of charitable fundraising (Mrs Bell was a particularly active supporter of the NSPCC, whose local branch met at the Hall for committee meetings and other events for many years) and of course, of cricket. Mr Bell was County President from 1972 to 1977 and after his death Mrs Bell was elected for 1978/9.The tradition is carried on in the 1990s by their son Mr John Bell, captain of Denbighshire in 1973 and President in 1995, who with his wife now occupies the Hall and continues to offer the family's well known hospitality to cricket lovers. The highspot of his own playing career was undoubtedly the early 1980s when Marchwiel twice, in 1980 and 1984, won the Whitbread Trophy for village cricket at Lords, and put the village and the ground well and truly on the map under his captaincy.

Cricketing Landmarks

1851 Mr Townshend Mainwaring, MP, JP, elected President of Wrexham Cricket Club
1863 Mr Samuel P Hope elected President of Wrexham Cricket Club
1883 The 'Marchwiel Square' created by Mr Piercy — the same year as the Ashes
1885 Mr Piercy's XI played Somerset
1886 Mr Piercy's XI played Wrexham Cricket Club
1892 First charity match. Proceeds used by Mrs Piercy to endow beds in Piercy Ward
1914 Mr Alfred McAlpine elected President
1922 Memorial Pavilion opened
1923 First Cricket Week
1924 Grand Charity Match — Mr Alfred McAlpine's XI vs Lancashire
1926 Jack Hobbs' partner Andrew Sandham appeared in Cricket Week
1928 Inauguration of the McAlpine Cup — Rhos won the first final
1931 South American XI at Cricket Week
1947 Lady McAlpine elected President
1951 Mr A J McAlpine's XI vs the Arabs XI (including Swanton, Allan and Peebles)
1961 Mr A J McAlpine elected President
1977 Death of Mr Peter Bell — memorial plaque erected

1980 Whitbread Trophy final at Lords — Marchwiel defeated Longparish
1984 Whitbread Trophy final at Lords — Marchwiel defeated Hursley Park
1991 Death of Mr A J McAlpine — Mrs McAlpine elected President
1994 Minor Counties match — Wales vs Cornwall
1995 Minor Counties match — Wales vs Wiltshire

The 1997 season included fixtures with Australian touring sides, all of which resulted in wins for the host team. Over the years since the late 1930s many players of international repute have visited Marchwiel, from Gubby Allen and Harold Larwood before the war, to Basil d'Oliveira, Bill Edrich, Jim Parks, Garfield Sobers, Ossie Wheatley and Sir Frank Worrall.

The Office of High Sheriff

It is not widely known that the office of High Sheriff of Denbighshire has on many occasions been conferred upon gentlemen of Marchwiel and district; as so many of them lived at the Hall, I have included their names in this chapter.

1585	Henry Parry of Maesglas (Greenfield) and Marchwiel
1588	Owen Brereton of Borras
1598	Edward Brereton (died in office succeeded by Robert Sontley)
1608	Morgan Broughton Esq
1611	Robert Sontley
1648	(another) Robert Sontley
1682	Joshua Edisbury
1697	John Hill Esq of Sontley
1698	Sir Edward Broughton
1743	Aquila Wyke Esq
1789	Charles Browne Esq
1805	Samuel Riley Esq
1840	Townshend Mainwaring Esq, MP, JP
1848	Simon Yorke Esq
1871	Samuel P Hope Esq
1895	Philip Yorke Esq
1923	Sir Alfred McAlpine
1934	R Stewart Brown Esq of Bryn-y-grog
1937	Simon Yorke Esq
1973	Peter Bell Esq

5: Sontley, Edisbury and Yorke

The study of Marchwiel's records over several centuries reveals many surnames which recur constantly, both amongst the prosperous and the poor of the parish. Three of these names stand out, however, because they were closely involved not only with village life but also with the wider interests of the county and even further afield.

The oldest of the three names is that of Sonlli or Sontley, and we must return here to the fourteenth century, to the three bardic brothers, Ednyfed, Madog and Llywelyn, who were the sons of Gruffudd ab Iorwerth, Lord of Sonlli and Eyton Uchaf (Upper). Ednyfed, the eldest, was the great-grandfather of Robert Wynn Sonlli, and from his time onward — about the middle of the fifteenth century — we can trace the direct line, confirmed by property deeds and, later, parish records. The family had several branches, in Esclusham, Cristionydd (Penycae) and Ruabon for example, and all these were consolidated and enlarged as the years went by, but this account is mostly confined to their Marchwiel connection.

The family home was Sontley Hall (Plâs Sonlli), which we know to have been occupied in the reign of Queen Elizabeth I by John Sontley, who may have built, rebuilt or extended the house. He was the eldest of ten children and his initials can still be seen on a magnificent overmantel which frames a blocked up fireplace. One of his brothers was Hugh, who became Rector of Marchwiel in 1556 and Vicar of Wrexham ten years later; he was an active Puritan and was closely involved in the trial of Richard Gwyn, the Catholic schoolmaster who was put to a hideous death on Wrexham Beast Market in 1584.

The Sontleys frequently called their eldest sons Robert; we have already met two, and there were to be four more, so there is a real danger of confusion especially when dates are not available. Robert Sontley's name appears twice as High Sheriff of Denbighshire (1598 and 1611) and his son Robert also held the office in 1648, just after the first Civil War. The family had benefited from the misfortune of a distant relative who had forfeited his lands for refusing the oath of loyalty imposed on all Catholics after the Gunpowder Plot in 1605, and had enriched itself considerably with those lands. In addition to this, the Robert Sontley of the Civil War period had apparently quarrelled with the church authorities (whether or not in Marchwiel we do not know) and turned as a result to the more extreme wing of Puritanism. In November 1641 he married Ursula Corbet of Longnor, near

Shrewsbury, youngest daughter of a leading Shropshire family, and their first child, Anne, was born at Longnor in 1643 when the war was at its height in North Wales and the North West. After the execution of the King in 1649, Robert Sontley and other Puritan gentry served on the County Committee which controlled civil, military and ecclesiastical government in Denbighshire throughout the 1650s. Robert died in 1657 leaving a son, another Robert, not yet of age; we can assume therefore that the Sontley lands were managed by Mrs Ursula Sontley, who cannot have found it an easy task. Her letter of 1657 to her husband's brother-in-law, William Edisbury (who had married Mary Sontley) asks for legal assistance in a case which she fears will be brought against her in the Assizes by one Bostock — almost certainly concerning a property dispute. I have not discovered the date of her death, but she was living in 1659 when she entered into an agreement with John Puleston 'of Havod y Werne, Gent', on behalf of her son Robert. It appears that the Sontleys had the right of burial in the North Aisle of Wrexham Parish Church and that John Sontley of Esclusham had been duly interred there, with Ursula Sontley's agreement, to the annoyance of Mr Puleston, who also claimed the right. He agreed, however, 'not to bury any person or persons on that side of the said Chancell claimd by the family of the Sonlleys until such time as the sayd Robert Sonlley shall attain to his full age of one and twenty years ...'.

It was probably thos Robert who (perhaps surprisingly in the light of the previous sentence) was buried in Ruabon on October 6th 1669, although another of the same name died in Marchwiel in July 1673. Whichever of them was the head of the household, he left a small daughter Anne, the last person to bear the Sontley name. In 1690 she married John Hill of Shrewsbury, who was nearly twenty years her senior, and they had two sons, Thomas and John; unfortunately Anne died in 1698, three weeks after John's birth. Her husband had already been Mayor of Shrewsbury and in 1697 was also High Sheriff of Denbighshire. Both of them are buried in St Chad's Church, Shrewsbury, and yet their contact with the parish of Marchwiel must still have been close for John Hill to have presented the magnificent silver Communion chalice and paten bearing the date of his death, 1731.

Some years previously the family had built a second home at New Sontley and John Hill is known to have been living there in 1715, so that any future references to Sontley must mean the new house. Edward Lhuyd remarked in 1699 that 'Sontley Park has now only some few pales standing about it', but he does not give more detail. Anne Sontley's son Thomas Hill (1692–1734) married the daughter of Dr Elstob, Dean of Canterbury and is himself buried in the Thomas a Becket Chapel of Canterbury Cathedral. He left extensive estates, not only in Marchwiel but also in Lodge, Brymbo, and elsewhere, but it is unlikely that he had much, if any, personal contact with the village, since in 1723 the Sontley Hall estate passed out of the family when it was conveyed to Richard Wynne of Herts. and William Myers

Worthy Sir:
I desier you woulde be pleased to speak
to some on that if my name be in question
it ont assies they maye answar for me and
I shall alow them theare fees as is dew
unto them. I cannot tell of any unless Bos-
teck shewed. he prates much and I feare
him littell. not elce but to tell you wee
are bound to pray for all our enimies
awld mrs Broughton was prai'd for in
our church this daye. and the collonell
did weepe very much it is to be feared
it will breack his hart. so god send us
a mery meeting I will not saye at
the funerall

          your sarvant

          Vrsula Sontley

my harty desiers and wellwishes
for my cosens former helthe

Letter written by Ursula Sontley, 1657.   *[The National Trust/Flitshire Record Office]* of London, in consequence of £3,000 lent to Thomas Hill by Susanna Letten of London. There were children of the marriage of Thomas and Matilda Hill, but by the 1760s it was Mrs Hill's trustees who were mortgaging and leasing out much of her Denbighshire property and in 1766 New Sontley was leased to David Roberts of London, Esq, (son of Henry Roberts of Llay, a Dissenter and a member of the Chester Street Congregation) who later bought it outright for £5,500. In 1772, however, he sold it to Philip Yorke I for £7,900, so that when Mr Yorke became one of the Marchwiel churchwardens later that year, he could be described as "Mr Philip Yorke of Sontley". The plan to be found among the Erddig papers shows a very elegant and formal looking house and gardens; it was described in 1759 as including '100 oak trees worth £730, 16 ash trees worth £20 and 257 lime trees worth £150'. The estate consisted of 146¼ acres, partly in Sontley and partly in Marchwiel, and ownership also included the best seat in the chancel of Marchwiel Church and 'the liberty and property of burial ground in the said Chancel as the Sontley and Hill family have heretofore enjoyed'. Wrexham's church registers contain the names of at least thirty Sontleys who were baptised or buried in the middle of the seventeenth century and some, at least, must have had connections with Marchwiel through their cousins.

Before we can study the Yorke family's contribution to this history we must first note the part played by their predecessors, the Edisburys, who came originally from Edisbury in Cheshire. At some point in the sixteenth century they began to use this surname in place of the original, which was Wilkinson. Richard Wilkinson or Edisbury held lands in Bedwell in 1544 and his son Robert acquired Stryt-yr-hwch through his marriage to Jane, daughter of Kenrick ap Howel. Their son Kenrick Edisbury bought Pentre Clawdd, Ruabon, which later passed to the best known members of the family, John and his two sons Joshua and John; it was John senior who bought the Erddig estate. Over the last twenty years or so these events have been so well documented by the National Trust and others that it is unnecessary to repeat all of them here: I shall therefore confine the details to those affecting Marchwiel.

In 1608 John and Kenrick Edisbury leased from the Crown a holding called Tythyn Hoell (Howell) at an annual rent of 20s 11¼d, and at about the same time Kenrick Edisbury seems to have gone to London, where, as a protege of Sir John Trevor of Trevalyn, he worked for the Navy Board and where he also met many Wrexham men; he had ready money to invest and they, it seems, were short of the same, so he was able to buy out several of them or allow them to mortgage their estates to him. One of them was his mother's cousin, Robert Powell. At home, Bedwell and Stryt-yr-hwch were the nucleus of his little empire, and in 1630 he also purchased Pentre Clawdd. In London his entrepreneurial skills apparently brought him to the attention of King Charles I and in 1632 he was made 'Surveyor of all our shipps' at a salary of £40 per annum, plus 4s for every day that he attends the said

Old Sontley Hall. The older part of the house is located behind the gable in the centre of this photograph.   *[W Alister Williams Collection]*

office on sea or land, and £8 per annum for his 'cochire' (coach hire). He had been living in Deptford, on the lower reaches of the Thames, for more than twenty years, and his father Robert had died there whilst on a visit in 1610. This was not a good time to have any dealings with the Stuart navy, which was in an advanced state of disarray, and I have not discovered what Edisbury reported to the King, but Charles was soon to cause outrage among country gentlemen by imposing the notorious 'Ship Money' tax, which he claimed was intended to improve the state of the navy. Whatever the success or otherwise of Kenrick Edisbury's new appointment, he was able in 1634 to buy the Toll and Tollage of the town of Wrexham and leased the King's Mill at a yearly rent to the King of £20 13s 4d. He died in about 1638 and there is a memorial to father and son in the parish church of St Mary in Chatham, the dockyard town at the centre of the Navy Board's operation

In about 1653 Kenrick Edisbury's son John bought the Erddig estate from Richard Davies, a citizen of London but almost certainly a man with Wrexham connections. It consisted of '13 messuages, 6 gardens, 6 orchards, 2 water corn mills, 300 acres of land, 60 of meadow, 200 of pasture, 50 of wood, 50 of moor and 40 of heath and bruery', in 'Erthig, Sontley and Marchwiel'. John Edisbury had almost certainly been a Royalist during the Civil War, and was captured by Colonel Mytton's force at Bangor Isycoed in 1643, but by 1646 he was Myddelton's steward

Gruffydd ap Iorwerth = Gwenhwyfar daughter of Madoc ap Llywelyn of Eyton
Lord of Sonlli
(early 14th century)

Ednyfed = Lleucu (Lucy)

Llewelyn Llogell Rhyson
Rector of Marchwiel in 1359

Madog Benfras

Llewelyn = Angharad daughter of Ieuan ap Meredydd ap Gruffydd Lloyd of Yale

Morgan Sonlli = Elin daughter of Iorwerth ap Ieuan

Robert Wyn Sonlli Hên (The Elder) = Elizabeth Brereton (died 1545)

Robert Wyn Sontley of Sontley = Elizabeth Puleston of Hafod-y-wern
(Living 1550)

John = Catherine daughter of David Lloyd (alias Puleston) of Cristionydd
(Living 1560s)

7 others

Hugh
Rector of Marchwiel 1556
Vicar of Wrexham 1566

Jane = William Edisbury

Robert Wyn Sontley = Gaynor daughter of Morris ab Ellis of Clenennau
(Living 1596)

Robert Powel = Jane
Vicar of St Martins 1589

Robert Sontley = Alice Fowler
(Living 1626)

Mary = William Edisbury
(died 1667)

Robert Sontley = Ursula Corbet of Longnor, Salop
(Dead by 1657)   1641

1666/67
= Elizabeth Hewitt of Shireoak

Robert Sontley
(Buried Ruabon 1669)

Anne Sontley = [1] Edward Mytton of Halston
(1669–98)   (Died France 1688)

[2] John Hill of Shrewsbury
(1650-1731)

Thomas = Matilda Elstob
(1693-1734)

John a Portugal merchant
(1698-1723)

Anne
(1691–1751)

Charles
(Died 1780)

John
(1725-57)

Anne

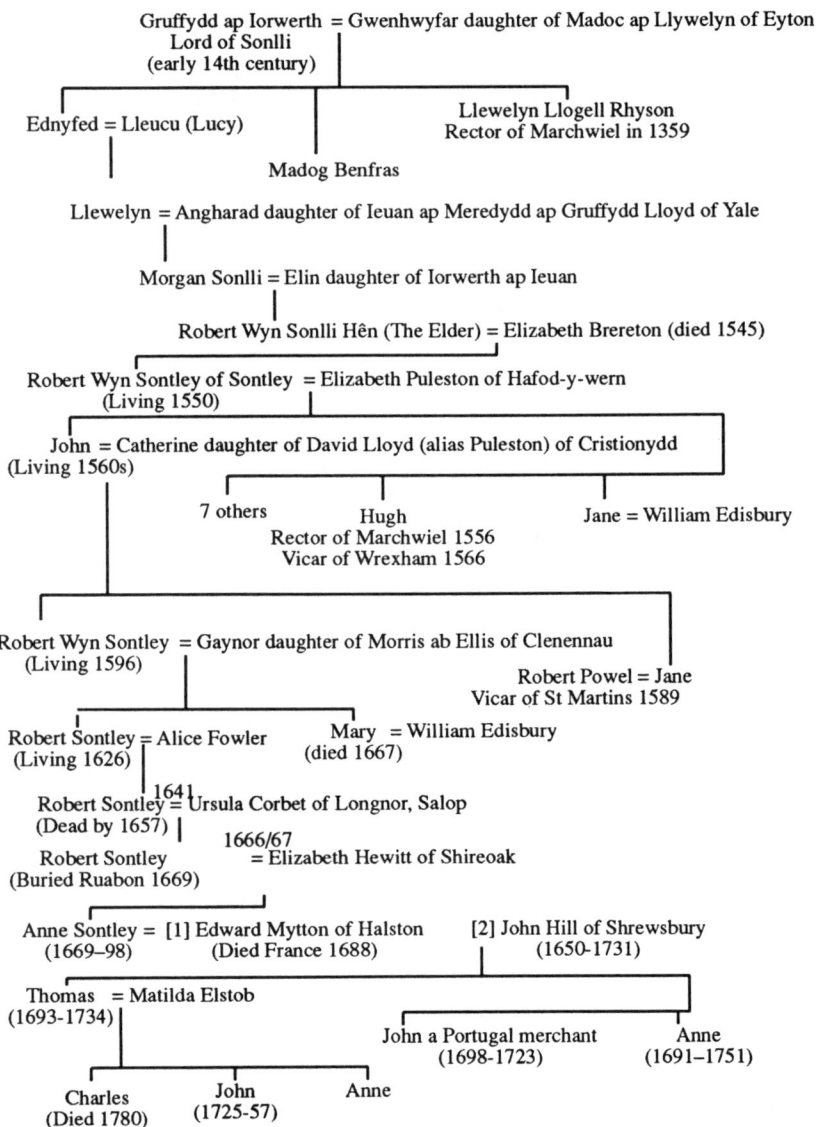

Pedigree of the Sontleys and Hills of Sontley

at Chirk and a Justice of the Peace in 1648/9 when a maimed Parliamentary soldier was awarded a pension. He married twice, and the story of his second wife Christian or Christiana, is worth repeating. She was the daughter of Sir Thomas Myddelton of Chirk and had first been married to Sir Roger Grosvenor of Eaton, Chester, the ancestor of the Dukes of Westminster; unfortunately he had been killed in a duel on Chester Racecourse by Major Roberts of Hafod-y-bwch. In 1661 John Edisbury moved into the house at Little Erddig as the country settled down under monarchy again, and seems to have lived there uneventfully until his death in 1677. In the previous year, as a beneficiary of the marriage settlement of Mary Tyler of Wrexham and George Ely of Wrexham, draper, he had acquired Bryn-y-grog, Marchwiel. The estate included Cae'r Groes, Cae'r Gegin, Yr Erw, Bryn-y-llan, Maes-y-llan, y Weirglodd, Erw'r Fynwent, Cae Glas and a parcel of land called the Pinfold.

His son Joshua built the nucleus of the present house at Erddig in the 1680s, but it is well known that he was an incompetent businessman and undoubtedly overreached himself, speculating in coal and lead mining and hardly ever paying his bills in full. In 1685/6 he leased Stryt-yr-hwch to Thomas Wright, yeoman 'of Streetyrhouch in Bedwall, parish of Marchwiel' at a rent of 40s for the duration of the lives of Wright's sons; one of them, Matthew, farmed there until his death in 1753. In 1691 on the other hand, Joshua bought up Joseph Dymock's estate in Sontley — Cae Nest and Tyddyn Conyn ap y Gof — for the sum of £830, but he never paid up in full. He borrowed from all and sundry, including Elihu Yale of Plas Grono and his own brother John, whose financial ruin he brought about. Despite all this, Joshua was apparently a jovial and popular figure in the locality. From 1709 onwards he was renting out part of Erddig; Rev Thomas Holland, who sometimes assisted in Marchwiel church, was a tenant for about five years.

The property was sold to John Meller in 1718 after five years of negotiations, during which the cautious lawyer had commissioned a survey giving him a comprehensive picture of his neighbours (including Sir Edward Broughton) and their assets. Joshua's death was reported, from somewhere in London, before he could sign the deeds of conveyance; the exact circumstances are not known, but he left no direct descendants. A sad end for a man who had been High Sheriff of Denbighshire in 1682.

The less flamboyant side of the family was represented by William Edisbury of Marchwiel and his son John who married Rose in Marchwiel Church in the early 1660s. Their eldest son William (b 1662) sold Cae Gwilym to Meller in 1725, whilst his brother Joseph was one of the churchwardens in 1709 and his signature appears often in the Vestry Book. Much later, in the nineteenth century, the tomb of various members of the family in the old churchyard was adorned with a metal plaque stating that 'this plate was restored by James Edisbury of Bersham, Gentleman, the representative of the ancient family of Edisburys of Erthigg AD

1855' and the family arms can be seen as one of the eighteen incorporated in the Yorke window.

John Meller was a good friend to the parish after moving into Erddig and seems to have been a shrewd but kindly man, who supported the earliest charity school in Marchwiel, run by the Society for the Propagation of Christian Knowledge, one of whose patrons he was. The Rector, Dr Ffoulkes, wrote to him on one occasion to say that that the parishioners 'are desirous to have a meeting at Marchwiel ... to agree about the rates of teams etc ... We should be glad if you can conveniently honor us with yr company and advice'. A question had obviously been asked about the possibility of christening a black servant, whose portrait, in livery and carrying a coach horn, can be seen at Erddig. It has been thought that he was Meller's servant, but this letter makes it clear that he worked for Major Roberts - possibly Meller's brother-in-law: 'I know no reason if the Major send his Black to me today, but he may be christened that morning ...' As we do not know the servant's name, it is not possible to check whether he was in fact baptised.

After John Meller's death in 1733, the Erddig estate passed to his nephew and executor Simon Yorke, and here began the link between the church and the Yorke family which was only brought to an end with the death of Philip Yorke III two and a half centuries later. Actually the house and park at Erddig are not in the parish of Marchwiel, but as the estate was consolidated with the purchase of New Sontley and other land, the squire became liable for his share of the dues and taxes which Marchwiel landowners were obliged to pay, especially tithes. Simon's son Philip, having given generously towards the rebuilding of the church, had by 1782 become involved in a dispute over financial responsibility for the new chancel, and hoped that Rev Samuel Strong would call a vestry to discuss the question.

On February 10th 1783 he wrote to his lawyer: 'Will you give me leave to state somewhat at large the following case and to request of you to transport the same to Mr Twigge who I am satisfied will do Mr Browne and myself the justice to give us such information as is in his power ... In the year 1776 Mr Browne, Mr Ellis and myself agreed with a Builder to re-edify the Chancel of Marchwiel Church for the sum of £119. It was accordingly completed to the contract and Mr Browne, Mr Ellis and myself ... pay'd him each the third of the expence amounting to £39 13s 4d.... at this time the property of the Chancel was supposed to rest in four parties viz', (the three named gentlemen and a Mr Twigge, who had not kept his word). The reply was not, perhaps, unexpected — Mr Twigge had sold his lands in Marchwiel, which lay next to the Marchwiel Hall estate, and his interest in the church had therefore ceased.

In the meantime Mr Yorke was served by his stewards, the two John Caesars, father and son,who ran the estate during his absences in London and elsewhere. In 1756 John Caesar the elder and his wife Margaret, who had married in the parish church of St Martin's, are recorded as living at Pentre Meilyn, part of Philip Yorke's

Wilkin Edisbury

Richard Wilkinson
of Edisbury, Cheshire

Robert Wilkinson alias Edisbury = Jane daughter of Robert ap Robert ap Howel
of Stryt-yr-Hwch   (Died 1618/19)
(Died 1616)

Kenrick Edisbury of Deptford & Bedwell
(Died 1638)

John Edisbury of Pentre Clawdd & Erddig = [1] Martha Downing   [2] Christian Grosvenor
(1608-77)

William Edisbury
(Living 1639)

John = Rose

William   James   Edward   John   Joseph
(Born 1662)   (Born 1663)   (Born 1665)   (Born 1667)   (Born 1670)

Joshua Edisbury of Erddig = Grace Delves
(Died c1718)

Dr John Edisbury
(Died 1713)

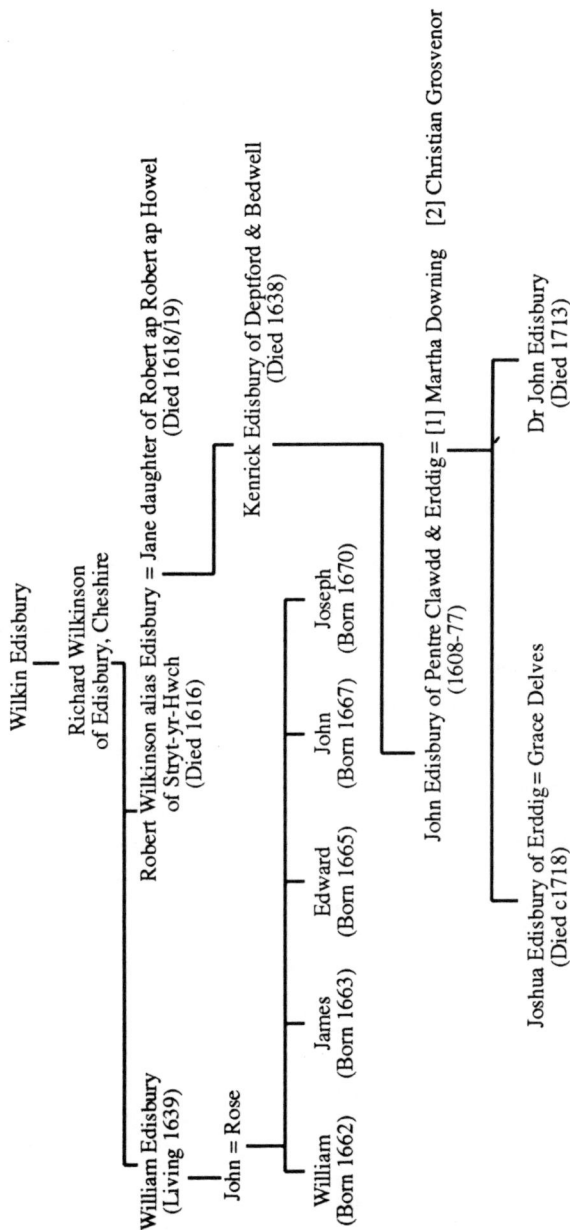

Pedigree of the Edisburys of Pentre Clawdd, Erddig & Marchwiel

estate. Caesar, like his master, was a churchwarden more than once, and was buried in Marchwiel in 1779; poor health had forced him to hand over his estate duties to his son several years earlier and Mr Yorke wrote to him in January 1775 expressing his regret at the death of Mr Anwyl and his urgent need to reach an agreement with the new incumbent about the Sontley tithes.

> Between ourselves, I pushed the Bishop hard for the living a month since, but it was long promised It would have been very desirable to have had a friend seated there.

As things turned out, the new Rector was a man after the squire's own heart. Rev Samuel Strong was in background as English as Mr Anwyl had been Welsh, but he was interested in history and the classics and became a frequent visitor to the Hall. The squire presented him with regular gifts of fruit and sweetmeats for himself and his family; for example in September 1778 he sent a gift of venison to the Rectory, and in 1780 he informed John Caesar that 'I will get Nelly to make some Raspberry jam & Currant Jelly ... and I wish Nelly to ask Mr Strong's children ... one day to Erthig and she and Betty Thomas will take care they do not make themselves sick'. Twenty years later one of these children, George, acted as his father's curate. In his turn the new Rector encouraged Philip Yorke in his study of the classics. For a man with no Welsh blood whatsoever, Philip became totally absorbed in Welsh culture and history and indeed he is best known for his major work of antiquarian history, the *Royal Tribes of Wales*, published in 1799. There is no doubt that Marchwiel Church benefited from the good relationship between the two men.

Mr Yorke wrote again to his steward in June 1775:

> By Mr Strong's letter ... I understand he has complied with the request of the parish and has appointed John Cross the clerk. As this man is somewhat among the rest indebted to my interest, I hope he will be diligent in your directions to him, to keep the pews clean and (if he has a Chest) to lock up the cushions of my own seat, having well brushed them, at such time as the family is absent, and that in regard to the monuments, he does no more to them than to brush off gently the dust or Cobwebs with a Fowl's wing, or such gentle thing, and that he does not officiously wash them with water, or use soap, all which would ruin the polish and delicacy of the marble. I would have you gravely communicate these instructions to him early, and tell him that if I find them regularly obeyed, I shall make him an annual present....
>
> I hope you continue careful and a good manager in the article of small beer, and see that the Door of the Cellar is kept locked, and the key never entrusted into improper hands: I am not willing to believe that the Brewer makes it stronger in my absence; If he did and you detected it, I am satisfied you would see it with the greatest and a proper indignation, and acquaint me of it, as well as any advisers or Encouragers of such a scheme ... I desire that ... you minutely attend the Brewer, and see that the small beer be of no increased strength whatever to what it was in my

Dear Brother .... Chester May 10th 1768

I should have wrote with the drawings which set out on Thursday last but for the hurry of the races. I went to all the Assemblys and liked them very well, they were vastly full every Night. I hope you receiv'd the Sea-Fowl safe, the reason of its being Quick, Mamma had sent for it, but, upon seeing your letter to John Jones, order'd it away immediately. Mr Pennant has beg'd of Mamma to let Betty Ratcliffe coppey for him, from a print, the youngest of Lord-Hardwicke's Daughters. Betty would be much oblig'd to you if you would get a Sheet of the finest grain'd white Vellum, and send it down by the Fly, as soon as possible Mamma Desire her Love to you, and Accept the same from;

Dear Brother, your Affect. Sister,

Anne I. Yorke

I beg you will give my Duty to my Uncle; when you see him; I hope he was not Displeas'd at my Accounts.

Letter written by Anne Jemima Yorke to her brother, 10 May 1768, about two years before her death. [National Trust/ Flintshire Record Office]

Father's time and the usual order of the house. Any irregularity of this sort, surreptitiously creeping in, must be attended with the worst consequences.

My wife, I thank God, and the children continue vastly well.

I remain
Your friend and wellwisher
Ph: Yorke

It is most likely that Caesar Bank, now part of the Marchwiel Hall estate, was named after the steward, and the last Philip Yorke told a most interesting story to the *Wrexham Advertiser* in 1956, which is worth repeating almost word for word, since it recalls his own unique brand of dry humour. The story concerns the unfortunate Reynold(s), who is believed to be buried under the triangle of grass which bears his name; as a suicide, he would not have been permitted to lie in consecrated ground.

My father told me that he knew a road-mender who had walked in the funeral procession of Reynolds, who had hanged himself in the wood somewhere up by Caesar Bank near where the "General Post Office" now is (a jocular term for the Victorian letter box, now no longer in use, opposite the top of Woodhouse Lane) ... I rather wonder whether the name may have had something to do with John Caesar, who was the trusted henchman of my great-great-grandfather Philip Yorke ... The roadmender said that they carried Reynolds down the lane and buried him at the crossroads which is not a crossroads and they drove a stake through his heart to prevent his ghost from walking. The object of the crossroads, I take it, was that should the stake fail to penetrate the heart, it was still a three to one chance against the ghost walking in your direction. But in the case of Reynolds it seems that the ghost would have no doubt as to which way to walk but back to Caesar Bank, the scene of his suicide.

Imagine the inconvenience of this for the good rector of Marchwiel as he returned after evensong past that point to his distant rectory ... It is, however, a well known fact that no ghost will pass a point in the road where a cross is clearly marked, so a cross was carved on the wall, and when we were children we used to get out of the pony cart and look for it, though I cannot remember now exactly where it was or what it looked like ...

What happened was that when the cricket field came into being at Marchwiel Hall, a part of the wall was reconstructed and another part of it was heightened, and the stone with the cross on it seems to have been turned round and the cross has disappeared inside the wall. Now I have no other evidence for stating this, but it seems to me that a cross is just as effective to a ghost when placed inside a wall as if it were clearly visible to the human eye on the outside. At any rate, I have not heard of Reynolds as having been seen beyond that point of recent years.

I do remember, though, my father telling me that there lived at one time at the Brook House, just below Reynolds Grave, a man whose name was, shall we say, Arthur. When pubs in Wales were closed on a Sunday, he was in the habit of

John Meller of London

John Meller of Erthig
(1665-1733)

Anne Meller = Simon Yorke

Simon Yorke I = Dorothy Hutton
(1696-1767)   (1717-87)

Elizabeth Cust [1] = Philip Yorke I = [2] Diana Meyrick (née Wynn)
(1749-79)   (1743-1804)   (1748-1805)

Anne Jemima
(1754-70)

6 children

Simon Yorke II = Margaret Holland
(1771-1834)

Simon Yorke III = Victoria Cust
(1811–94)

Philip Yorke II = Louisa M Scott
(1849–1922)

Victor Joseph Yorke
(1857–81)

Simon Yorke IV
(1903-66)

Philip Yorke III
(1905-78)

Pedigree of the Yorke Family of Erddig

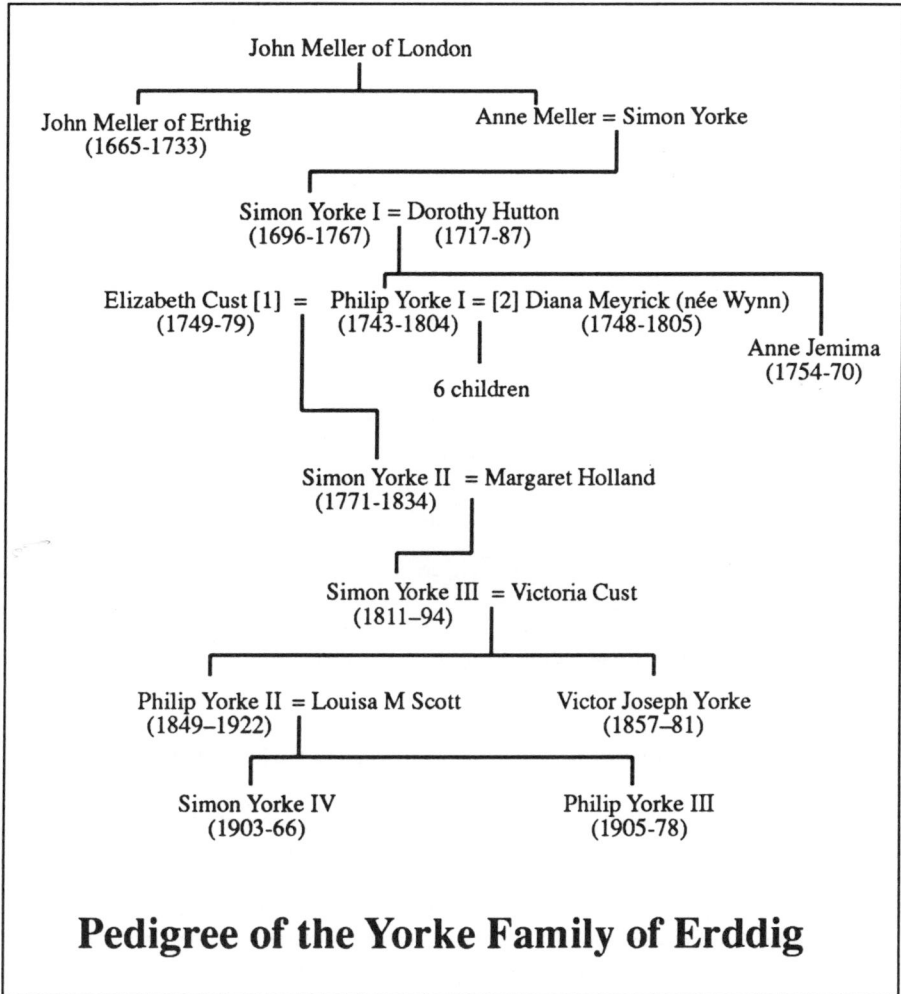

returning home by a different route from his usual one from the Waggoners at Gyfelia, and he never failed to give Reynolds a cheery 'Goodnight' as he passed his grave. But one night his 'Goodnight, Reynolds' was answered by a sepulchral 'Goodnight, Arthur', from deep down among the bushes. And Arthur ran headlong down the hill, which was steeper then than it is now, and over the bridge which was more humpbacked then than it is now, and into the cottage like lightning, bolting and barring the door behind him. When he related his terrifying experience to his workmates, he was surprised to find that they treated the matter with more levity than he expected, and suggested that the voice might have been that of one of his mates

Marchwiel Rectory, 1816. From a drawing by Moses Griffiths. [National Library of Wales]

who wanted to see whether he was capable of winning the hundred yards race in the oncoming sports.

A more recent and more probable appearance of Reynolds seems to have been in connection with a horse which my brother had before the war. This horse could not have been expected to know much about the events which took place there before he was born, coming as he did from halfway down the Vale of Clwyd; and yet, however tired he was on his way back from hunting, or at any other time, he always took the trouble to 'shy' whenever he passed that point after dark. My father was born 107 years ago (*ie* in 1849), and supposing the roadmender to have been something over seventy years old when they met, it would put the date of Reynolds' suicide as somewhere about the year 1790. And I rather hope that I may one day see a figure clad in the garb of the late eighteenth century seated upon that fine new concrete bench which a thoughtful council has erected there. And then if he can point out to me the exact position where the body lies, and if any remains are to be found, I daresay that by now quite a good case could be made out for having Reynolds re-interred in Marchwiel churchyard ...

The parish records contain references to the baptism and burial of several Caesars, and clearly John and Margaret could not resist the obvious temptation when naming another of their sons, Julius Caesar, who was buried in Marchwiel in 1764. In 1818 Thomas Caesar, stated to be of Hafod-y-bwch, was buried at the age of 62, and his wife Hannah followed him in 1837, aged 78.

Philip Yorke I died in 1804 and it was Marchwiel's Rector, Samuel Strong who wrote his obituary for the *Gentleman's Magazine*. It is significant that his heir, Simon II, commissioned one of the finest sculptors in the country, Richard Westmacott Jnr, to produce his memorial (see Chapter 1). He was later to become famous as the creator of the Waterloo Vase which stands, all twenty tons of marble, in Buckingham Palace, and in 1827 he was appointed Professor of Sculpture at the Royal Academy. Simon II, also played a part in the ongoing additions to the church and churchyard especially in the 1820s; it was he whose agent received the letter of complaint about all the expense. He was approached in 1823 by the Bishop of St Asaph, father of the newly appointed Rector, Rev J H Montagu Luxmoore, on the subject of land for the proposed new Rectory. The Rector had written to his father as follows:

My Dear Lord

I Inclose you a plan of the glebe at Marchwiel near the Rectory house. Owing to the disposition of the ground, it is of great consequence (should I build near the present site, which I am anxious of doing) that I sh'd possess myself of a small slip of the adjoining field belonging to Mr Yorke and let to Vaughan. There is close to the village of Marchwiel near the Red Lion Inn a parcel of land measuring one acre which is wholly surrounded by Mr Yorke's property and let to Davies - except on the road side, to which it is contiguous.

This I sh'd be happy to exchange with Mr Yorke for the land which is pencilled in the inclosed plan. The use I shall want to make of it is chiefly for a road - none of it will be built on - but small as it is, it would be a great acquisition to the Rector. I understand Mr Yorke is in y'r present neighbourhood, and sh'd you deem it expedient to interfere in this, the business may not only be facilitated but hastened.

I am unwilling to begin building till I know whether I c'd exchange this land. Sh'd I get a decided promise of exchange before the 28th of this month, Penson w'd peg out the ground for me on the 29th and he assures me if we begin the foundations before the first of September the house may be covered in before the frost.

I am
Your very affect. son

J H Montagu Luxmoore
Marchwiel, August 17th 1823

The Bishop carried out his son's request and wrote to Mr Yorke, who replied in September 1823, courteously but very firmly, directly to the new Rector:

My dear Sir

Having looked over my two fields adjoining the Rectory House at Marchwiel, I find that the acre which you propose taking from them would be of great disadvantage to the farm - under this consideration you must excuse me for not accepting your offer of an Acre of Glebe Land near the village in exchange, which I think would not be an equal compensation for the loss of such valuable old pasture land. In respect to your other proposal to take a spot 30 yards by 15 situated under a hedge and high trees from this land, I must require from you a quantity of the Glebe land in exchange equal to the value of this spot with the Timber for the accommodation which I am willing to grant.

I remain Yrs
Simon Yorke

This was a copy which Mr Yorke kept of his reply, and on the reverse a note says that Well Field, adjoining Vaughan's farmhouse, (the present Bentley's Farm) consists of 2 acres 1 rood 11 perches. The correspondence appears to have ended here!

Simon Yorke II was also a Trustee of Tyddyn Daniel, and is commemorated, with his wife Margaret, nee Holland, in two of the windows in the chancel of the church. In 1834 he was succeeded by Simon III, who presided over the Erddig estate for sixty years, almost exactly contemporary with the reign of Queen Victoria. In 1846 he married one of the Queen's godchildren, Victoria Cust, and seems to have spent most of the time on his estate, unlike his more cosmopolitan predecessors. He cared deeply for his properties and his tenants, and was regarded with real affection in the area. By now Mr Yorke was the most substantial landowner in the parish and built several farmhouses, such as Pontyffrwd in its Victorian red brick, and modernised others. Again there was a very close and friendly link with the Rectory; in 1852 Mr Luxmoore presented to Erddig's library a copy of Wycliffe's New Testament of 1360, while a few years later Mrs Yorke, a skilled needlewoman, presented the church with a fine altar cloth.

In 1877 Simon's elder son, Philip, married Annette Puleston, an occasion marked by the schoolchildren and their master, Mr Nind, with the presentation of an engraved photograph album. Unfortunately the marriage was disastrously unhappy and shortlived and Philip spent almost twenty years travelling abroad and then working in the East End of London, fearing the criticism of Denbighshire society and heedless of his father's pleas for him to return. One feels great sympathy for the family at this stage; Simon's second son Victor was serving in South Africa with the Royal Engineers during the Zulu and first Boer Wars. Two or three of his letters still remain, and one of them refers to the tragic death of the Prince Imperial, son of the exiled Emperor Napoleon III of France, who had asked to be allowed to serve in the British Army.

Victor Joseph Yorke in the uniform of a cadet at HMS Conway, *prior to obtaining a commission in the Royal Engineers.*

(From Zululand, May 14th 1879) ... dear mother, in future you must never be anxious about me - first because I am like a bad halfpenny, sure to turn up all right somewhere, and secondly because it is quite time to be anxious when you see my name among the killed, not among the missing, mind ... Of course by this time you will have heard of the death of the Prince Imperial ... it happened three miles form our camp on the Inyotyozi River ... the prince and escort ... had off saddled their horses and had lunch on the edge of a donga bounded by a mealie field. As they were about to start again a volley was fired at them by 7 Zulus concealed in the mealies. Nobody was hurt but it seems to have caused a panic for they jumped on to their horses and rode as an Irishman would say 'like devils in a high wind', except the poor prince, whose foot slipped and whose horse got away from him, and one trooper and a Basuto who it is to be hoped lost their lives in trying to save his, not being in such a hurry as the other cowards.

This tragedy was followed by more than one courtmartial back in Britain, and it is interesting to read Lieut. Yorke's first hand account. Shortly afterwards he wrote to his father:

> I have just lost my pony Taffy ... he used to follow me like a dog and let me do anything with him and has many a time carried me over places where an English horse would break his own and his rider's neck. It is supposed he ate some poisonous grass during a short halt ... Afterwards he died quite quietly with his head in my lap .... .
>
> Believe me ever your very affectionate son
> Victor Yorke

One of Victor's last letters was to his mother, describing the capture of the Zulu king Cetewayo and remarking upon his own career prospects. He hoped to get a commission but felt that in any case the colonial army was best for him — 'long leave and better pay, the only way to get on in the army nowadays unless one happens to have brains enough to pass the Staff College, which I haven't. With best love to all, Believe me, Ever your very affectionate son, Victor J Yorke.'

A year or so later, on April 6th 1881, this likeable and unassuming young man was himself killed by a shot from Basuto pickets, as the memorial behind the clergy desk in the church tells us. He was buried in South Africa and his heartbroken father, who had inherited the family's fondness for writing verse, expressed his feelings as follows:

> When tidings came from out the town
> Which filled our hearts with sore distress.
> It seemed as if the sun went down
> And ne'er would rise for our redress .
> It seemed the ending of all joy
> When the news came of our dead boy.
>
> He died that day which marks my birth
> The next eve saw him closed in earth.
> I shall ne'er see his peaceful grave,
> Yet know he rests among the brave:
> The brave who fell in a just cause,
> While thus fulfilling England's laws.

Simon Yorke III was a man of great humanity who was deeply shocked when in August 1880, a few months before his son's death, there was an accident at Bersham Colliery, which had been operating since 1867 on his land and within sight of the windows of his home; nine men, including the manager, were killed. He wrote: .

> I fain would 'fuel up' with wood
> And chop it all my life:
> If by such means I haply could
> Make accidents less rife.

By the 1890s there was much talk of disestablishing the Anglican Church in

Wales, although this did not actually take place until 1920, and concerned meetings were held up and down the country. Simon Yorke was a passionate opponent of what he saw as an attack upon the church itself. Disestablishment, he wrote, would 'separate the Church from her constituted guardian, the State, and would enable that State to become the 'wicked uncle' in the tale of the Babes in the Wood ...' One of his speeches was apparently delivered in Marchwiel, where another new Rector, Rev John Sturkey, had become a personal friend. For this occasion he wrote:

> Ladies and Gentlemen, A great crisis is at hand, or I would not have ventured at my time of life to do myself the honour of coming into your presence as Chairman of this meeting ... Now that the Church is in danger, all Nonconformist and Christian Liberals have an opportunity offered them of shewing their true faith in Christ by defending the Church of England, for she is their true mother in Christ, and they are all her children, and have as much right in her as any churchman has, whether he be rich or poor, great or small ... Is it not reasonable to suppose that should the Church be despoiled of her rightful property, the property of all Nonconformists and even the Roman Catholics who are also our fellow Christians, should meet with the same fate?
>
> There is no sin in being a Nonconformist, for it is the misfortune, not the fault of those who are thus situated. [Not quite so humane this time!] But there is sin in wrong and robbery ... particularly when done under the cloak of piety ... A Conservative Welchman thus sends greeting to his fellow Christians, the Nonconformist Liberals of North Wales.

Another of Mr Yorke's interests was to copy out in detail Mr Sturkey's sermons after hearing them in church, and he kept a careful note of the date when manuscripts were received at Erddig, and when they were copied. When he died in 1894, his son Philip Yorke II continued his father's interest in the village - both were active school Managers and the children were regular guests at tea parties and other treats at Erddig. In 1902, his estranged wife having died in 1899, Philip married Miss Louisa Scott, and one of their first joint appearances in the village was a visit to the school in September.

The new squire was of course anxious to maintain and increase the profitability of his estate, and in May 1905 details were given to him, as an interested party, of the New Calyx Drill and Boring Company's plans to bore for coal on Fitzhugh land, between Bryn Newydd and Old Llwyn Onn. If work had gone ahead, a mine railway would have been built from Bersham, crossing north of Sontley and Stryt-yr-hwch across to Woodhouse Lane, traversing the village just north of the present Post Office, and on to link up with the Wrexham–Ellesmere line in Abenbury. (Large sections of the line would have been underground, of course, with only a very short stretch visible on the landscape). The option was extended to March 1908, and there exists a lease drawn up between Philip Yorke and the Plas Power Coal Company Ltd in August 1911, with an accompanying plan showing the position of a geological fault running under Crabtree Green and just West of

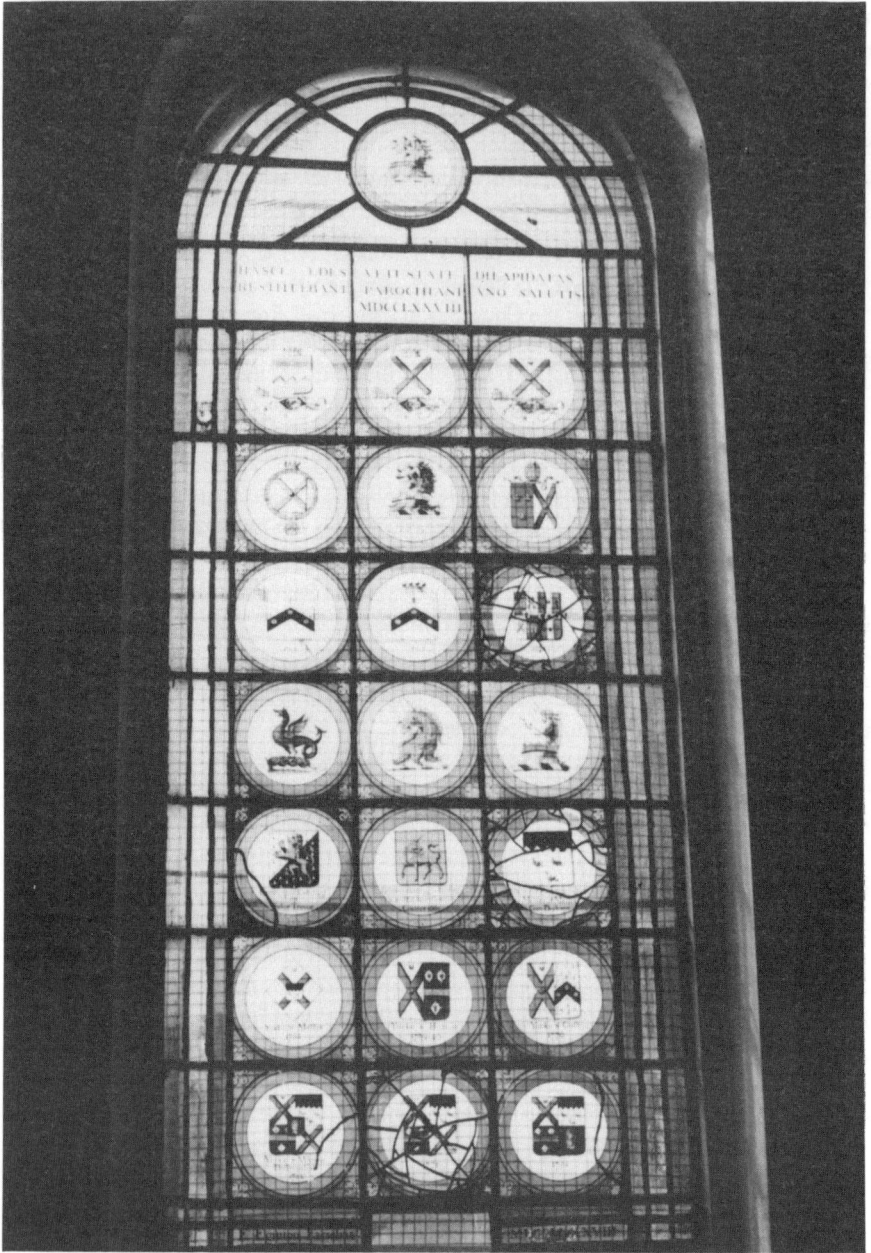

The Yorke Window in Marchwiel Church.   *[W Alister Williams Collection]*

Marchwiel Hall. Whether for this or for other reasons, the lease was never signed and no more was heard of the plan. In the period following the First World War and in the early twenties some of the Yorkes' land in the village was sold for building, especially plots between the Post Office and Maes-y-llan, as well as some farmland, as the family decided to realise some of its capital.

In 1907 another new Rector was appointed — Canon Fletcher of Wrexham, soon to be Archdeacon also. It would appear that the traditionally friendly relations which had existed between squire and parson now came under some strain, especially when in 1908 plans were announced to refurbish the church by removing the box pews. Through his solicitor, Philip Yorke opposed the plan tooth and nail, and as it happened the idea was temporarily abandoned, but worse was to follow. Mr Yorke died in 1922 leaving two sons still under twenty one, so it was the newly widowed Mrs Yorke who heard to her horror in 1923 that all the oak box pews installed by William Worrall in the 1770s were to be removed and replaced by others in pitch pine. Many of the tenants apparently supported her protest and she even appealed to the newly created Archbishop of Wales, Dr Edwards (who was also Bishop of St Asaph), but he was unable to accept her argument and her solicitor advised her that as she was not actually resident in the parish, she had no official position from which to oppose the changes. The plans went ahead and the Erddig pew and its cushions were removed and taken to the Hall. Three years later some of the new wood was found to be suffering from dry rot, which must have caused the family a certain grim satisfaction, but their offer to replace the diseased pews with best oak, provided that their own was returned to the church, was not taken up. Further distress was caused in the 1940s when the wartime need for metal dictated the removal of the ornamental chains around family burial plots, and the last Simon Yorke had to be assured that this was a national rather than an ecclesiastical requirement; Mrs Yorke died in 1951 and is buried beside her husband after what must have been a very sad period in the family's history.

In the 1950s and until his death in 1966, Simon Yorke IV was seen occasionally in the village, usually on horseback inspecting his farms, whereas his younger brother Philip lived at Plas Noble and, later in Ruabon, before inheriting Erddig in due course. Even before that time, however, he was a good friend to the school, where he gave out the prizes in 1949, and the church, where he had a standing arrangement with Canon Thomas that if he was present at Morning Service — and he invariably arrived on his bicycle after it had begun, he would read the lessons from the lectern, which incidentally is very similar to the one in the family chapel at Erddig. His very effective speaking voice and his cheerful personality made him popular throughout the district, and in 1973 he brought Erddig to the attention of the whole nation when he gave his estate to the National Trust, including of course the properties in Marchwiel and Sontley. Five years later the last of the Yorkes died very suddenly just before the start of morning service, not in Marchwiel,

surrounded by the memorials to his ancestors, but in Penylan, where he had decided
to worship that day having left too little time to cycle the extra few miles. His
funeral service in St Marcella's church a few days later was attended by several
hundred people — village residents, estate workers and National Trust
representatives among them, and his memorial, erected in 1981 by the Trust above
the pulpit pays tribute to him as a loyal churchman. As it happens, it is situated next
to that of the first Simon, John Meller's nephew, who had died in 1767; Philip
himself once said that a man could wish for no better epitaph than that of his great-
great-great-grandfather — 'A pious, temperate, sensible country gentleman of a
very mild, just and benevolent character, as the concern for his death did best
testify; an Advantage which Amiable Men have over great Ones'. We may well feel
that these words applied as much to the last of the Yorkes as to the first.

6: Landscape and population

Before the end of the seventeenth century our main source of information about
the geography of the village is the large number of deeds, probably running into
hundreds, relating to mortgages, leases and re-leases of land and houses, but from
them we learn little or nothing of the individuals concerned. We have already heard
of the almost totally Welsh pedigrees of most of the inhabitants in the Middle Ages
and the Tudor period; a century later in 1699, Edward Lluyd and his associates
conducted a survey of the parishes of Wales, printed under the title of Parochialia,
and the entry for Marchwiel makes fascinating reading, in a mixture of English and
Welsh as follows:

> Marchwial (Denbighshire), distant from Wrexham one mile and a half, situate in
> ye Hundred of Welsh Maelor, surrounded with ye parishes of Ruabon, Wrexham
> Gresford and Bangor. The Length from Pentre Velin Bridge [*ie* Kings Mills] on ye
> border of Wrexham to ye Stone Bridge on ye border of Bangor a mile and a half. The
> Breadth o'r Pumryd ar derv. Gwrexham i'r Kroesae Gwnnion ar dervyn Bangor yn
> Vilhdir [from Pumrhyd on the border of Wrexham to the White Crosses (see Chapter
> 1) on the border of Bangor, one mile]. By ye church are 5 houses and a little
> Smithie...
> A Rectory, Mr Thos Smyth of Chirk; ye curate Mr Charles.

> Houses of Note (Y Tai Kyfrifol)
>   1. Marchwial Mr Edw Broughton
>   2. Sonlhe bel: to John Hill Esq of Shrewsbury in right of his wife Anne ye

Daughter of Rt. Sontley Esq.
3. Street (Stryt) yr Hwch Hall bel: to Joshua Edisbury Esq of Erdhig
4. Marchwiail bel: to Edward Brereton Esq
5. Ibid Will. Edisbury
6. Sontley Ph. Roberts (worth) 14 pounds p'ann
7. Bryn y Grog, Mrs Elis of Wrexham. here stood an old Cross.

Sontley Park has now onely some few pales standing abt. it
Sir Edward Broughton has a Warren adjoining to his hall.

Rivers.
1. Klywedog Spr. part. at Mwynglawdh (Minera), partly at Rhiwabon and mears (or divides) ye parish from Wrexham.
2. Bydrog rises a little above ye Gereliae in Rhiwabon and falls into Klywedog a little short of Pentre'r velin (*ie* Kings Mills) above ye bridge.

The Bridges
1. Pont Koed y Glyn on Klywedog 2 miles and a half above its fall into Dee.
2. Pont Pentre'r velin half a mile lower.
3. The Stone Bridge in Bangor.

Their Well, at Coed-y-glyn. Their fuel, Coal. They have plenty of Marl [clay] through Maelor Saesneg.

Lhuyd ends with a snippet of personal interest — 'Edward Dymmog (of Sontley) burried 8 years since (actually July 1686) was near 100 years old'. This Edward Dymmog, or Dymock, served as a juryman at the Court of Great Sessions in Wrexham in the late 1650s.

We have already considered the plight of the poor at the beginning of the eighteenth century; the more fortunate parishioners, whether gentry, farmers or tradesmen, continued to be assessed and taxed, for various purposes, according to the value of their property, and these lists are a vital source of information until the census returns in Queen Victoria's reign. A list of freeholders dated 1741 is headed by the Rector, Mr Anwyl, and also includes two Edisburys, Aquila Wyke Esq of Llwynegryn, Matthew Wright of Stryt-yr-Hwch, and Rev Mr Parry of St Martin's near Chirk (this involvement came about because the parish of St Martin's in 1734 bought Berthen Gron in Sontley, and rented it to tenants at £50 per year, a sum which was used to assist its own poor; the nearby St Martin's Cottages, no longer standing, were also let for the same purpose). A note explains that Rev Mr Holland, though resident in Marchwiel, was actually a Wrexham freeholder. (See reference to him in Chapter 1) Mr Holland's activities in acquiring property throughout the district would make a book in themselves; in his will he left property called 'Sputty' in Wrexham (Ysbyty was the area now covered by Queen's Square and the corner of Rhosddu Road, where the old Public Library and the Glynn Cinema were built) to his niece, Elizabeth Trygarn, said to be 'of Marchwiel'; perhaps she had looked after him at Marchwiel Hall after the death of his wife. (Mrs Trygarn was also believed to be a fervent Jacobite). In 1784 a later Rector, Rev Samuel Strong, leased Ty'n Twll from Philip Yorke I at an annual rent of £18, but even without this property he would have been liable, because of his glebe land, to pay the Land Tax imposed in the late eighteenth century on Marchwiel and Sontley; he heads the list at £4, followed by Wm Youd at £3 2s 0d, Widow Ednyfed at £1 2s 7d and Mr Edgworth of Bryn-y-grog at 12s 9d. For twenty years this tax yielded the same amount — £63 2s 4d - and in 1780 we find Charles Browne of Marchwiel Hall paying £5 9s 4d and Philip Yorke (for the first time) paying £2 7s 0d in respect of his Marchwiel lands. For his Sontley property he was assessed for £4 14s 8d out of a total of £20 15s 4d. There was one very unusual argument in 1779 — Daniel Tunnah appealed on the grounds of being confused with Daniel Owens of Pentre Meilyn and undercharged 3s 5d!

Some useful details are provided by the clergy in their replies to the questions of the Bishop or Archdeacon, who regularly conducted their Diocesan Visitation. The handwritten replies can be seen at the National Library in Aberystwyth; in his 1791 return Mr Strong reports that his parish is 'about 8 miles in circumference and comprehends 73 houses and 82 families. The only house of note is that of Charles Browne Esq, occasionally resident'. He goes on to say that only one farmer and his family are non-Anglicans, assembling in a 'licensed place at Wrexham' for Presbyterian worship. Fifty years earlier, Mr Anwyl had been asked, concerning such families, 'what endeavours are used to convince them of their errors?' but both Rectors seem to have found their Nonconformist parishioners to be 'People of a decent and orderly behaviour' and therefore left them in peace. In this connection, it should be remembered that throughout the nineteenth century Salem Chapel in Sontley served the needs of local Presbyterians, but it was closed in 1966 and has now become a private house.

We move next to the tithe details of 1843, where we find an alphabetical list of all landowners and tenants in the parish, including the very poorest, and with a most detailed map produced at the same period. Mr Luxmoore most thoughtfully had his tithe records bound in leather for the use of this successors, to say nothing of students of local history. He knew to the last halfpenny how much was due to him over the year — the total amount of tithe-rent would be £636 with a variable addition based on the last seven years' corn prices. Richard Birch of Kiln Farm heads the alphabetical list, assessed for £9 16s 2d; William Bradshaw of Tyddyn Daniel for £5 19s 7d; John Evans of Top House £8 15s 8d; Thomas Davies of Old Sontley £2 19 7½d; John Morris, The Groves, £26 5s 7½d; Mrs Wainwright of New Sontley £56 8s 7d; Daniel Williams of Highgate (demolished later in the century — it lay beyond the end of The Ridgeway, not far from Holly Hedge) £16 2s 7d; at the other end of the scale Wilkins of Bryndedwyn paid 7s 3½d and Charles Prince of

Glebe Cottage 3s 8d; James Ellis from one of the cottages near Gwrych Teg was charged 2s 3½d.

This charge fell upon the tenant of property rather than the landlord, and it became a severe burden at the time of the great depression in agriculture forty years later. In 1891 the law was changed to make the landlord rather than the tenant responsible, so the demand in Marchwiel fell chiefly upon the Erddig estate, with the Kenyon, Fitzhugh and Williams Wynn estates also bearing their share.

The tithe map is, as in the case of Highgate, a valuable source of information on the farms and cottages of the village which have now disappeared, since we have their exact positions in addition to their mention in the census returns. Bryndedwyn Cottages lay along the lane between Kiln Farm and Sontley Mill and Smithy, a route which was in living memory a very busy thoroughfare. Several farms are, confusingly, called simply Marchwiel, but from their position we can identify Bentley's (also variously known as Croes-y-mab and Vaughan's Farm), Penyllan, The Cottage and Top House.

Although the ten-yearly census was first carried out in 1801, it was not until 1851 that its findings relating to Marchwiel were sufficiently detailed to be helpful to the general reader. We do have a summary of the earlier statistics, however; out of a population of 493 in 1801 — 89 families occupying 76 houses — 435 people were employed in agriculture and 43 in trade and manufacture. Thirty years later there were 79 families in agriculture and 9 in trade and manufacture — probably not a great difference. Fifty-six women worked as servants. By 1841 the village had grown and 553 persons occupied in 85 houses, whilst in Sontley there were 13 properties. In 1851, the year of the Crystal Palace Exhibition, deaths seem to have overtaken births, as the figure was down to 535 and it did not recover until 1871, when there were 598 recorded inhabitants. The census enumerators of 1851 began with the Bryn-y-grog end of the village with Pentre Llwygedd Cottages, a row of four on the bend at the bottom of the hill. They were demolished in the 1930s to improve the bend. Moving up to Croesymab there were two households — that of Thomas Woodhall, gentleman's butler, with his wife, 5 children and servant, and also George Kemp MD, consulting physician. In addition there was Croesymab Gate across the turnpike road, with a gatehouse whose keeper, Mrs Hannah Davies aged 26, collected tolls for the Wrexham and Chester Turnpike Trust. (She was still there ten years later with her husband Joseph, a groom, and 4 children.) Richard Birch and his family continued as the tenants at Old Hall and the Luxmoore family now occupied the Rectory, along with a butler, lady's maid, housemaid and dairymaid. In the National School House lived the master, Robert Roberts, a bachelor of 27 whose sister acted as his housekeeper. At number 3 Cock Bank Cottages lived the coachman at the Rectory, John Jones. Continuing into Sontley, the census enumerators passed along Stryt-yr-hwch, and it is interesting to see in 1851 the rare use of its English name, Sow Lane, the Welsh form being much more common, even when mis-spelt as 'Street-yr-Hwch' in the now Anglicised village. Whoever drew the map spelt Welsh names as he heard them — Pentre Mailyn, which appeared variously over the years as 'Milin' or 'Mylin' now becomes 'Moilin', whilst Berthen Gron is rendered as Perthlangron. (Easily the most imaginative rendering of a Welsh name, however, must be one map reference to Brynycabanau; it appears as 'Binicumbani'!). At Sontley Smithy lived James and Martha Morris, the blacksmith and his wife who ran a dame school in her front parlour, while at Stone Cottages Isaac Garner, aged 18 and described as a railway worker (perhaps at Johnstown or Ruabon) lived with his grandparents. At Old Sontley the widowed Eliza Davies farmed 296 acres and brought up six young children, albeit with the help of six servants.

The other part of the parish, to the north-east of the turnpike road, was more sparsely populated, with only a third of the total inhabitants, although it included what we should regard as the heart of the village, near the church. Gibraltar Cottages could boast a Chelsea Pensioner named William Jones, who was visiting his old home, whilst Highgate House, owned by Lord Kenyon was farmed by Edward Davies. Five Fords (also now demolished) was tenanted by John Parsonage and Pumrhyd by Charles and Elizabeth Clutton who had six children under the age of thirteen. Top House Farm, with its lovely old barn, had 129 acres; the whole site was sold and cleared in the 1960s when The Ridgeway and Deiniol Avenue were built. We are rather hampered by the fact that nineteen properties in the village centre were referred to only as cottages, without further detail; the only identifiable one is The Cottage itself, where Mr Meredith Evans farmed 115 acres. In 1851 he had four sons and two daughters, whilst ten years later his family had grown to eight. The 1861 enumerator also mentions the brick barn opposite the top of Station Road, which was used by the Evans family as an Independent Sunday School within living memory, although it too was demolished for road improvement in the 1960s. Meredith Evans's descendant, Miss Evans, lived in the house until the 1950s. The other cottages were the rows along the main road from Smithy Cotttages opposite the present Post Office down to the church.

By 1861 the Rectory was occupied by the Rev Stephen Donne and his family. He had five children aged between seven and twenty-nine, and in addition the living-in servants included a cook, nurse, housemaid, kitchenmaid and groom. (The last Philip Yorke told the story that one of the Misses Donne was dancing at a party at Erddig, held in the present Music Room, when the ribbons on her dress got ever more tangled up in the handle of the brand-new mechanical organ as she whirled this way and that, and she eventually had to be unwound!). The schoolmaster was again Elias Jones (he had served before 1851 but appears to have left the post for a while); his 20 year old son worked as a book-keeper at Kings Mills. At Croes-y-mab, next on the list so we must assume that it is the present Bentleys Farm, were John and Hannah Roberts and their son John, a wheelwright, while at the 'other'

Croes-y-mab, lived Edward and Mary Cheetham. There was also a lodger, a retired curate Rev John Hoskins. There was a tollgate at the other end of the village also, at Cock Bank, where the gatekeeper was William Gittins, whilst at Cock Bank Cottages, one of the three houses was home to a couple with two children, an elderly brother, a boarder and a 'nurseling' aged 11 who was described as a cowboy. Near the junction of Stryt-yr-hwch and the Overton road was a cottage known as the Barracks, for unexplained reasons — it appears on the detailed Ordnance Survey map of 1872. At Sontley Mill were the Jones family, the miller and his wife and five children, whilst at Sontley Smithy lived John Griffiths the blacksmith, born at Pumrhyd, as well as his wife, eight children and a servant. Marchwiel Smithy was in the hands of John Edwards, and the population also included a brewer, David Price. New houses and cottages were constantly being built at this time, although not all have survived. We get addresses like Field Cottage or The Fields, and in 1891 there was even The Village Shed, occupied by John Downes, of the same family as Thomas Downes, murdered half a century earlier. Fifty years earlier, the list of the poor had included several who inhabited The Birdsnest, of which we know nothing more. The 1881 census is the first to refer to Bentley's Farm as such, the occupants being Richard Cliffe and his family. Mr Cliffe was to be one of the first Parish Councillors a few years later. In Cock Bank cottages we find the village's only coalminer, who would have had a cross-country walk to one of

Rev Montagu Luxmoore's Rectory (now the Old Rectory) c1910.   *[Mrs A Hamlett]*

several pits in the Ruabon/Bersham area. The new school in the village was now in operation, but there was still no house, and the master, James Nind, lived in one of the Bangor Road Cottages with his wife, four children and a young servant. In one of the cottages opposite the school lived George Fisher, a rolled leather dresser, with his young wife and new baby daughter, who was to be the future Mrs Samuel of the Post Office. On the Overton Road at Pontyffrwd we find a shoemaker employing two men — Griffith Roberts, born in Dolgellau — and people would walk several miles to have their boots and shoes repaired.

The enumerator for the census of 1891 (the latest whose details are open to the public) was the Headmaster appointed in 1886, Mr A A Walker, who with his young family lived in the new School House in the centre of the village. By 1891 Grove Cottage and Cheshire View had been built, and the village was beginning to take on the appearance it would have presented in the 1920s, before the housebuilding phase which filled most of the land to the East of the main road. As the new century opened the population stood at 626 and there were 135 houses in the parish. In May 1911 the Royal Commission on Ancient Monuments sent its officers to Marchwiel to make their report. We have already heard their comments on the mediaeval crosses, and they also turned their attention to several local farms. About Kiln Farm in Sontley they say:

> Stretching South from the stackyard at the back of the farmstead into a field still called 'Moat Field' is a broad ditch about 90 yards long by an average of 12 yards wide. It appears at its southern end to have once turned West and would thus partly enclose the present stackyard; but only one side of the moat now remains. The existing house was built in 1804.

Unfortunately no light can be shed upon the age or purpose of this ditch, and the present owner feels it is much more likely to have been connected with the brickmaking activities of the neighbourhood, as there is clay at the bottom of it. The Commissioners also visited Old Hall, and had this to say:

> Directly to the East of the farmyard of the present Marchwiel Old Hall are the remains of a moat which apparently once enclosed the site of the older house and what is now an orchard. The length of the moat, extending North and South for a distance of 60 yards, is still in much of its original condition, and of an average width of 20 feet; the sides at right angles to this length are also clearly evident for about 40 yards, but the water has disappeared and the moat has been partially filled up. The fourth side towards the present farm buildings has disappeared. The area of the enclosed space is about half an acre.

Little is known of the original house referred to by the Commissioners, but it is believed to have been a mediaeval manor house, of which there are still visible some traces in stone. We do know that it was probably the present house, a fine example of Georgian architecture, which was occupied by Richard and Mary Birch, who were buried in Marchwiel in 1781. Successive generations of Birches played a prominent part in village life — another Richard occupied the farm in 1861 — but they did not own the property, being tenant farmers for Thomas D Ellis, Esq. He left it in his will ('all lands etc called Marchwiel formerly in the occupation of Richard Birch') to the Poole family who came from the Whitchurch area. The new owner, Mr C H Poole, married in 1870 Miss Isabel Chetwynd, but her interest in the property was later cancelled and eventually, in 1892, it passed to Mr J W Evans and his brother and sister, changing hands only once more since that time. The map accompanying the 1892 transfer indicates some interesting field names — Parson's Field (separating Old Hall from the Old Rectory), Cae Bennet, Cae Bythell and Big and Little Trowster.

Thirdly, the Commissioners visited Old Sontley, which is in all probability the oldest building in the parish, with its original portions predating the church by almost two centuries. More is said elsewhere about the Sonlli or Sontley family who lived there from the sixteenth until the early eighteenth century, but the two outstanding features of the house are a splendid plaster overmantel above a blocked-up fireplace on the upper floor, bearing the initials 'I' (or J) 'S' for John Sontley, probably the first of the family to live there, and on the other side of the building an oak beam still bears its scriptural quotations.

New Sontley does not, as its name implies, have quite such a long history. The original house, whose construction date is uncertain, was occupied by John Hill of (Old) Sontley in 1715 and at the time of his death in 1731, and when his widowed

Part of the overmantel still in situ at Sontley Hall.   [W Alister Williams Collection]

Pentre Llwygedd Cottages at Bryn-y-grog.   *[Mrs Gwenda Kent]*

The gardens at Bryn-y-grog, c1910.   *[W Alister Williams Collection]*

daughter-in-law Matilda Hill showed no sign of wishing to live in the neighbourhood it was sold, passing eventually, in 1772 to Philip Yorke I, thus making him one of Marchwiel's parishioners. The house was rebuilt over the next few years.

Although the 1911 report confines itself to the places mentioned above, there are several other farms and houses of interest in the area.

Bryn Newydd is first mentioned in a deed of 1726 (Plas Power Estate) when Thomas Treen, yeoman, was granted an 11-year lease at £36 annual rent from Robert Ellice of Broughton, who in 1730 was raising a mortgage on the property, described as 'lately built'. It then passed to Miss Mary Myddelton of Croesnewydd, and upon her death in 1747 it was inherited by William Lloyd.

Bryn-y-grog, the site of the mediaeval cross, has a complicated history of ownership. Elizabeth, daughter of Cynwrig (Kenrick) ap Robert of 'Bryn y Grogyn in Marchwiail' married first Dr David Powel, vicar of Ruabon (died 1578) and later Edward Eyton of Ruabon. In 1676 the property passed into the hands of John and Joshua Edisbury as part of a marriage settlement, and it included Cae'r Groes, Cae'r Gegin, Yr Erw, Bryn-y-llan, Maes-y-llan, y Weirglodd, Erw'r Fynwent, Cae Glas and a parcel called the Pinfold. There is a strong tradition in the neighbourhood that hangings took place in the field between the present house and Marchwiel Hall Lane, marked until recent years by a copse of trees, and that this is the origin of the name — the 'hanging hill' (Welsh *crogi* — to hang or crucify). However, the noun *crog* can mean a cross or rood, and the name could be another reference to the mediaeval cross). In 1706 or 7 the property passed to Robert Hughes of Wrexham, Gent, (probably when Joshua Edisbury was desperately in debt) and by 1758 it was owned by John Jones of Wrexham, grocer and ironmonger. In a memorandum of 1772 he offered to hand over to John Edgworth of Bryn-y-grog, for a consideration of £51 '... all that messuage or tenement, croft and Garden ... on the West side of the Churchyard there, late in the holding of John Cross ... and also all that seat, pew or sitting place in the Parish Church of Marchwiel aforesaid situate in a western part of the (a)Isle of the said church to the North part of the Chancell and adjoyning to a seat of Aquila Wyke Esq on the East and to a seat of the said John Edgworth on the North and West sides thereof. To hold from the Tenth day of October next ensuing forever free from all encumbrances whatsoever.' This gives us a clear picture of a section of the congregation in the last years of the old church, but the document is unsigned. It appears that John Jones had already, in 1771, sold the house itself back to Philip Yorke I for just over £1,600, but clearly this was an earlier building than the present one, which would appear to date from the late eighteenth or early nineteenth century. Possibly Mr Edgworth only leased the property at this time. At any rate, he died there in 1798 and one of his family, Thomas Edgworth, served as the first Mayor of Wrexham when the borough was granted its charter in 1857. It is worth noting that the present Bryn-y-grog is not unlike the Old Rectory in appearance, so possibly it also was rebuilt in the 1820s, like its neighbour.

Five Fords Farm was originally part of Sir Watkin Williams Wynn's estate and among its internal features was a fine seventeenth century staircase. In 1892 part of the lease was surrendered and the property was eventually owned by Wrexham Borough Council, who, following a transfer in tenancy, decided to demolish it some twenty five years ago and replace it with two modern dwellings.

Highgate House, demolished in the latter part of the last century, lay between Top House and Holly Hedge. A sale prospectus of 1856 divided it into three main lots — (1) 8 fields totalling over 35 acres on the road from Bangor to Pumrhyd Mill; (2) the farm and 22 acres adjoining Fitzhugh land and occupied by George Williams and (3) 11 acres known as Cae Brown, next door to the land of Mr Evans, the Cottage.

The King's Mill dates from the very earliest times, but its modern history dates from its purchase in 1634 by Kenrick Edisbury. It then passed to the Yorkes, and it was Philip Yorke I who rebuilt it in 1768/69, to increase the efficiency of his enterprises. The mill was in operation until 1940 and gradually fell into a dangerous and dilapidated state until it was restored by Wrexham Council in the 1980s. It was built, and rebuilt, of stone quarried just a few hundred yards away in Abenbury, and this quarry is mentioned in Norden's Survey of 1620; the stone is of a pale greyish pink shade and was used extensively in the Wrexham area — for example to construct the viaducts on the Wrexham–Ellesmere Railway. In Philip Yorke I's time it was known as 'Mr Lloyd's quarry' in reference to William Lloyd of Plas Power, who owned Bryn Newydd, the adjoining property.

Pentre Meilyn or Mailyn is first mentioned in a marriage settlement of 1583 involving Robert ap David ap Gruffydd of Pentre Meilyr; clearly meilyr was the name of a mediaeval or early Tudor tenant. In the time of Philip Yorke I, it was occupied by his steward John Caesar and his wife Margaret, who married in 1753. They later moved to Bryn Goleu and Pentre Meilyn was leased to Daniel owens in 1769, at an annual rent of £32. The Owens family occupied the property for several generations, but it was sold by the Yorke family in the present century.

Pontyffrwd was also owned by the Yorkes (and often referred to in their papers as Pont-y-frood). Its name refers to the stone bridge just south of the farmhouse, and we should remember that the historic property is the one on the right of the Overton Road when leaving the village. (Its neighbour on the left is a Victorian addition by Simon Yorke III, although the tithe map of 1841 does indicate the existence of an earlier farm on the same site). The first document which I have traced is dated 15th February 1699/1700, when Joshua Edisbury leased the farm to John Roberts of Wrexham, yeoman, at an annual rent of 40s during his lifetime. The house has been modernised in recent years but still carries the unmistakable appearance of a late seventeenth century dwelling.

Pumrhyd (the original Welsh meaning Five Fords) is the name referring to both the farm and the mill on the eastern boundary of the parish, and both, in addition to appearing in parish records over the last three centuries, were mentioned by A N Palmer in his accounts of Wrexham and district and the end of the last century. The old cornmill was part of the Marchwiel Hall estate in the time of the Broughtons and remained so until it was bought by Daniel Dackombe in about 1842. Palmer's chapter includes an attractive sketch of the mill before it was rebuilt later in the century. The nearby farmhouse of the same name was owned by the Randles family in the nineteenth century (Thomas Randles, Surgeon, attended the poor in the 1820s, as we have seen in an earlier chapter) and in 1851 the property was occupied by Charles and Elizabeth Clutton and their six young children. The house has clearly been altered and extended as is proved by its seventeenth century rear aspect and eighteenth or early nineteenth century brick facade. One of Marchwiel's earliest preserved registers refers to Edward, son of Roger and Eleanor Griffiths of Pumrhyd, who was baptised on 7th April 1695, and almost two centuries later we find John Griffiths and his son Nathan, who were born there, serving both Marchwiel and Sontley as blacksmiths.

Stryt-yr-hwch lies just off the lane of the same name which runs from Reynolds' Grave to the Overton Road at Cock Bank. It was a well established property by the early seventeenth century when it was occupied by Robert Wilkinson alias Edisbury (died 1616) and his wife Jane daughter of Kenrick ap Robert ap Howel. They were

Pumrhyd Farm.   *[Mrs Edwina Theunissen]*

the parents of Kenrick Edisbury and it was probably their grandson John who leased it in the 1650s, after the Civil War, to Colonel Robert Broughton and his wife Mary. Shortly afterwards it was mentioned (as 'Streeterhough'), with other lands in Marchwiel and Ruabon, as part of the marriage settlement between Joshua Edisbury and Grace Delves. In 1685 or 86 Joshua leased it to Thomas Wright, yeoman, at an annual rent of 40s for the lifetime of Wright and his sons; in 1760 Elizabeth Wright, widow of Matthew Wright (died 1753) obtained from Philip Yorke a new lease for 28 years at a rent of £60, but four years later the remainder of the lease was assigned to William Youd. In 1796 it appeared in a list of properties bought by Lord Kenyon for a total of £23,870 and including Old Sontley itself, Sontley mill and the smithy. Edward Davies was his tenant in 1837, and later the farm was occupied by several generations of the Roberts family, who held it until recently.

Tanyllan Farm on the Overton Road was part of the Erddig estate and in 1837 was occupied by John Cheetham, another active local resident. The land consisted of 118 acres, stretching from the bend almost opposite the present Rectory, down as far as Pontyffrwd, and the original farmhouse was demolished to make way for the present Highfield Farm.

The Groves in Sontley is a most interesting example of an early 17th century farmhouse, with its timber-framed exterior to the rear, its Jabobean staircase and beams and its distinctive front windows. Bricked-up mullioned window frames in one of the barns indicate an even earlier house on the site. A valuation of landed property in 1837 gives the occupier as Thomas Jones, but the land has been farmed by the Morris family for well over a century, with succeeding generations representing Sontley on the Parish Council and also, prior to 1927, acting as Overseers of the Poor.

Not all the houses of interest are farms, however. In the centre of the village, next door to the present Marchwiel Garage, is Stone House with four adjacent cottages, all of which have been refurbished in recent years. During restoration a fireplace was revealed, bearing a late seventeenth century date, and of course this row of houses near the church is the one referred to as 'The Village' in Mr Luxmoore's lists of property, and in the census returns. It is highly likely that the whole row was at one time occupied by quarry workers. In the present century Mr Sam: Clutton and his family lived in Stone House — Mr Clutton was one of the first Trustees of the Piercy Hall and the Trustees' deed refers to him as a brickmaker; this brings to mind the brickworks which Messrs Collins and Son operated behind Brickyard Cottages on the Bangor Road earlier this century. There has always been plenty of clay in the area (we remember Edward Lhuyd's references to marl) and there are still in existence a few bricks carrying the identifying Marchwiel mark. There was an attempt to lease land attached to The Hollies for brickmaking in the 1890s, but this appears to have come to nothing.

We must not forget the *Red Lion Inn*, which played an important part in village life not only in the social sense, but also as a provider of suitable accommodation for various meetings such as the Vestry, until in the 1820s the additions to the church and the building of the first National School provided alternative locations for meetings. The property has been part of the Erddig estate probably since the time of the Edisburys, and it is certain that in the nineteenth century the landlord was frequently a retired servant of the estate, the best known example being Mr Cain Ratcliffe, formerly the Yorkes' coachman, who died in 1910 and was succeeded by his widow. It seems clear that the 'little smithie' which Edward Lhuyd described in 1699 as being near the church, was on the same premises, since in 1837 the landlord, Thomas Hughes, was also the blacksmith, while in 1841 the tithe map describes this corner site as 'house, garden, smithy and stable'. In external appearance the *Red Lion* still fitted this description until the 1960s, with its mounting block and cobbled yard.

This chapter on some of the buildings and residents of the past would not be complete without mention of the Dunbabin family of Gwrych Teg. Their former home is technically in the parish of Bangor, but they always played a prominent part in Marchwiel life, and were certainly listed for rating and tithe purposes. The first to be mentioned is Martin Dunbabin, who in 1656 witnessed the sale of a pew to Hugh Lloyd by John Edisbury. In 1677 one of the churchwardens was Henry Dunbabin, who reported to the diocese that 'as for marriages, we had none within

An excursion stage-coach outside The Red Lion *c1910,. the licensee, Mr Ratcliffe, is standing by the horses.*

the year 1677', nor in the next two years, as it happened; in 1682 he himself improved the statistics by marrying Mary Ralph. There must have been half a dozen or more of the family called John; in the eighteenth century they signed two of the Glebe Terriers, and by 1822 John Dunbabin was Vestry Clerk, commemorated by a tablet in the North Aisle when he died in 1828 aged only 50. It was his son, also John, who sailed to Tasmania in 1830 from Portsmouth. He settled in a small township called Bream Creek, thirty-four miles east of Hobart, in a property which he called Marchwiel Farm and it is very satisfying to know that the schoolchildren of the two communities have now begun to correspond regularly.

Another local name with connections in Marchwiel was that of the Rowland family, who were living in the area in 1662, when Margaret, daughter of Ellen and Thomas Rowland, was baptised. They were possibly related to a Major Rowland of Gerwyn, who it seems was a cavalry officer in Cromwell's New Model Army during the Civil War. There are eight or nine members of the family buried in the churchyard, including Edward Rowland of Llwyn Onn, who established himself as a druggist in Wrexham in 1810 but died at the early age of 38 in 1826. His wife Mary (née Langshaw) lived until 1852, but of their five children they lost a 30 year old daughter, Emma, in 1846, and in 1850 their third son Samuel, Chief Officer of the ship *Standard* of London, was lost at sea, also aged 30. The business was carried on by the youngest son, William at its premises at 9 High Street, only recently vacated after trading there since 1846. Mr William Rowland was Mayor of Wrexham in 1869 and his son Sir Leonard served four terms in office early this century.

We should always remember that there is much to be learned from walking around the older parts of any churchyard to find the last resting place of those who figured so prominently in the story of their locality. Undoubtedly a large number of those whose names appear in this narrative lie to the West and South of the church building, *ie* on the Bangor Road side, some in clearly marked graves, others anonymously by now. It is surely a matter of great regret that all physical trace of them vanishes when epitaphs can no longer be deciphered or, worse still, when their graves are vandalised and made unrecognisable. I hope that references in this book to some of the villagers of the past will help to preserve their memory, alongside the valuable transcription work which has been carried out on gravestones and parish registers by the Clwyd Family History Society.

7: Education

In 1738, the Bishop of St Asaph sent out one of his regular requests for information on the state of his parishes, this one being addressed to his 'good brother' Maurice Anwyl, who had recently become Rector. The second question concerned schools, and Mr Anwyl gave the following detailed reply:

> 2 schools; one of them is maintain'd by Madam Myddelton and Mr York, the former gives 40 shillings for teaching poor children, the lat[t]er two guineas towards cloathing them. The number of scholars are twelve. The other is maintain'd by neighbours who send thr children there to be instructed: twenty scholars only, 7 or 8 of this parish. At both schools care is taken to instruct 'em in ye Catechism.

The first mentioned was one of the charity schools opened by the SPCK throughout the country, and John Meller Esq of Erddig had been a very active supporter, and indeed even bequeathed his legal chambers in London to the Society; we know that the school existed in 1719, when Rev Humphrey Ffoulkes bought Bibles for the poor, since 'Mr Evans' received one 'for the use of the Charytye School'. Clearly Meller's nephew, Simon Yorke I, was carrying on his work. Miss Mary Myddelton of Croesnewydd, one of the Chirk Castle family, was a most generous benefactor in the Wrexham area, and John Hill Esq of Sontley had also helped financially until his death in 1731. By 1795 matters were not quite so encouraging; Rev Samuel Strong reported that,

> There is a voluntary charity school for twelve children, mostly supported by the Rector. Reading only is taught. They are neither lodged, fed not clothed. When they leave school the parents dispose of them as they please. There is also a Sunday School of about thirty persons, supported by contributions.

By 1799 the Sunday School was 'not very well attended' and by 1809 the churchwardens had to report that although the charity school still taught reading to about twenty children, the Sunday School 'was dropped last year for want of being attended. The Books distributed, besides Bibles, Common Prayers and Testaments, are several of the Tracts from the Society for Promoting Christian Knowledge'. The charity school was almost certainly housed in one of the glebe cottages near the church, and was run by one master, although Mr Evans' qualifications, and those of his successors, have not come down to us.

The next development came shortly after an Indenture had been drawn up between the Rt Hon George, Lord Kenyon, Baron of Gredington, and Rev J H M

Luxmoore, Clerk, Rector of Marchwiel in 1825. Lord Kenyon 'conveyed a piece of land suitable in the parish of Marchwiel on which a schoolhouse and school for the education of children in the principles of the Established Church of England and Ireland on the Madras or National system of education ... Nevertheless ... if the said schoolhouse and school should at any time thereafter, from neglect, dilapidation or otherwise ... cease to be used and applied for that purpose ... then the said premises should immediately revert to the said George Lord Kenyon and the grant should cease and become void'. We know something of the education which was provided in the little school across the fields from Marchwiel Hall and the Old Rectory, because it was visited on 26th January 1847 by the Commissioners for the notorious *Survey of Education in Wales in 1847* (known in Wales as the 'Treason of the Blue Books' because of its dismissive attitude towards Welsh culture) and received a comparatively favourable report:

> There are 553 inhabitants, all employed in agriculture. No Welsh is spoken. The Master was formerly a blacksmith and is now a gardener every afternoon and one day a week. Discipline etc, good. The school is privately supported by the Rector, except for the small amount raised by the children's payments. The building is clean, well warmed and ventilated, and in good repair.

The master in 1847 was Elias Jones aged 37, a native of Selattyn, who was paid a salary of £36 per year and also earned £1 10s 0d per year as Vestry Clerk, an office which he held until 1861.

The instruction was of course entirely in English, the girls being taught needlework in the afternoons, probably by the Rector's wife, whilst for the boys, school ended at 1 pm. There were 23 girls and 19 boys on the books (5 under 5, 25 aged between 5 and 10 and 12 over the age of 10) and on the day of the inspection there were 35 pupils present, being taught together in a room 18ft by 36ft in size. Nine children had been attending for more than four years and 17 for less than one year, and the morning lessons included Scripture and the Catechism, as befitted a Church school, and also reading. writing, arithmetic, geography and music. Although the Rector, Mr Luxmoore, supported the venture out of his own pocket, a weekly fee of one penny was charged, with the fourth child in each family admitted free. The Commissioner remarks that of the 35 children present, 8 could read with ease and write legibly on paper.

> There are maps upon the walls, but no books for teaching geography. 21 children could repeat the Catechism, but their knowledge appeared to be acquired by rote. The master ... has never been trained to teach and has received no education since he was ten years of age. He appears to take pains with his school, maintains good discipline and observes the rules of the school, which are strict as regards the Catechism, Collects, prayers and ritual of the Church with exactness and decorum.

Elias Jones had also appeared on Rector Luxmoore's list, drawn up in 1841, of the 'poorer persons' in the village, who lived in the School House with his wife and two children. (By the time of the Census of 1851, however, he appears to have abandoned his teaching, at least temporarily, since the schoolmaster in that year was said to be Mr Robert Roberts aged 27, whose young sister acted as his housekeeper.) It is also worth noting that there were two other establishments in 1847, of the type generally known as 'dame schools'; one was run by a Mrs Jones in her dwelling house, in a room of 15 feet by 12 feet into which 20 children could be packed, although on the day of the visit there were only eleven. I have not been able to identify the house, but Mrs Jones had been running her school for two years and earned £6 10s 0d in a year from the children's pennies. The inspection was comparatively complimentary to her, but not so fortunate was Mrs Martha Morris of Sontley Smithy, whose cottage room may have been larger (18 feet by 15 feet) and held a possible 25 children, but whose various facilities were described as inadequate or unsatisfactory. Mrs Morris, the wife of James Morris, the blacksmith, had been running her school for five years — indeed she was still teaching at the age of 70, according to the 1851 Census. In each of these establishments the majority of the pupils were in the 5–10 age group and all lived nearby, whilst about one third of those at the National School lived between one and two miles away. All children aged between six and twelve are described in the Census returns as 'scholars', and we must remember that they would have walked across several fields and lanes in order to attend, whether from the cottages near the church or from Cock Bank and Stone Bridge. Most, as we know, were the children of agricultural labourers, but we should also notice that Mrs Eliza Davies of Old Sontley, the widow of Thomas Davies, was a lady of considerable importance in the village — she farmed 296 acres and employed six workers, at the same time bringing up six children under twelve,who were probably pupils at the school.

Ten years later, by the time of the 1861 Census, the master was again Mr Elias Jones, who was back in the School House with his wife Mary, a governess, his 20 year old son William, who was a book-keeper at Kings Mills, and his daughter Louisa aged 13 and still at school.

In 1863, the new Rector, Rev Stephen Donne, was able to confirm that the buildings were being used for their rightful purpose, but that they were already too small and too far from the main village. They therefore reverted to Lord Kenyon in accordance with the deed of 1825, and were later sold to Mr Hope of Marchwiel Hall. In the 1950s they were converted into a modern house, but it is still possible to visualise the buildings as they must have looked when classes ceased.

Meanwhile plans were under way for a new school building, which was to be opened in 1874, but before that time elementary education had been transformed by the great Education Act of 1870. This created state schools unconnected with the Anglican Church, whilst at the same time the church schools were given a large measure of government financial support — in return for regular inspections by officers who reported to the Board of Education on the attendance, discipline, state of buildings and evidence of effective teaching. Failure to satisfy the inspectors in any of these respects could lead to withdrawal or reduction of the grant, and the school log books of the period contain regular references to the reports, copied out by the master in charge of the school. One of Marchwiel's first post-1870 reports, dated May 1873, says: 'This little school is beginning to get into working order'. The Inspector visited again in the Autumn, when 26 children were examined, 7 in Standard IV, 7 in Standard III, 8 in Standard II, 4 in Standard I and 11 infants. Just previous to this time the master in charge was Mr James Mantle aged 47, who was married with three children — Ernest aged 17 (described as a tutor) Laura (15) and Clara (14). All three were born in Gloucester, where he had met his wife. By 1873 he had been replaced by a certificated teacher, Mr James Nind, who was a native of Evesham; in the Census of 1881, seven years after the opening of the new school but before the building of a new School House, he is described as being 37 years old, with a wife and four children as well as a young servant, all living in one of the Bangor Road cottages opposite Top House Farm. Like several of his successors, Mr Nind appears to have played for church services, at least in 1874/5, for which he was paid £1 10s per year 'for the harmonium' and also served as parish clerk in 1882/83, at a quarterly salary of £3 10s 0d.

School attendance was officially compulsory, but this was in practice very difficult to enforce, especially in a rural area, and the reasons for the absence of many pupils, and indeed the frequent closure of the school, are quite revealing. Harvest holidays began in mid August, but if the gleaning was not finished, children were still kept away when school reopened in September. Other regular occurrences were the Wrexham Pleasure Fair, potato planting, acorn gathering, poultry dressing at Christmas, Bangor Races and the village wake. Tea parties given by the ladies of the locality at Erddig, Marchwiel Hall, Bryn-y-grog, Maes-y-nant and others, whilst inspired by kindness and generosity, must have involved quite a few interruptions to the timetable. Indeed later on, one inspector pointed out that forty weeks in a calendar year were necessary to fulfil the attendance requirements of the government's Code. Epidemics, of course, were the most serious reason for absence — measles and mumps were commonplace, but we also read of black typhus fever in Clwtt in 1874, so that 'school was closed against all scholars from that side of the parish'. March 30th: 'Opened school today after 3 weeks' vacation (because of the fever); attendance small; scholars gone backward during the time school has been closed'. The weather, of course, affected attendance very severely; many children still had to walk through fields or muddy lanes, and days of heavy rain or high winds are often recorded, with the few children who had arrived being allowed to leave early. Indeed the summer of 1879 was one of the wettest ever recorded, with crops rotting and farmers facing ruin; in Marchwiel there was snow on April 14th, and from May until August it rained incessantly.

By a deed dated January 22nd 1874, Rev W H Boscawen, Rector of Marchwiel, with the consent of the Bishop of St Asaph and under the authority of the School Sites Act, 'granted to the Archdeacon of St Asaph and his successors a piece of land forming part of a field called Erw'r Deial, bounded as described in the deed, which therefore formed part of the glebe land of the rectory of the parish ... to permit the land and buildings thereon to be appropriated for a school for the education of children or adults or children only, of the labouring, manufacturing and other poorer classes in the parish of Marchwiel, such schools to be always in union with the National Society ...' The deed gives 'the government of the school, the appointment and dismissal of the teacher and the selection of books to a committee consisting of the Incumbent, his curate and four other persons being members of the Established Church and subscribers to the funds of the School of not less than 10 shillings each ... The religious instruction in the school and the entire control and management of any Sunday School held in the premises, shall be vested in the Incumbent or, in his absence, in the officiating minister'. On February 9th 1874 the foundation stone for the new buiding was laid by the Rector and the Building Committee, and on September 7th Mr Nind could write: 'Commenced work after the holidays in the New School room in the village with an average attendance... .'

> Sept. 9th Holiday — opening of the new school. Teaparty for villagers and schoolchildren. Concert in the evening.
> Sept. 14th Attendance improved this week. Several new scholars and several left the school. Old scholars recovering from the holidays.

It is interesting to note that in 1874 the Managers had asked Mr Nind to draw the plans for the new school, and for this he was paid two guineas. The new building was in fact the top portion of the site now occupied by Mr Scott's furnishing store; the dimensions were described as follows: Main Room length 36ft, breadth 17ft and height 13ft; Classroom length 15ft, breadth 17ft and height 13ft. Mr Shone of Red Wither, the builder, was paid £379 16s 8d for his work. The red brick classrooms nearest the road were not added until 1894 and 1899.

It was expected by all concerned that the Rector would play a very important part in the running of this Church school, and in the late 19th and early 20th centuries the religious instruction of the children was entirely in the hands of successive clergy. We should bear in mind that up to 1874 they had a walk of only a few minutes down the lane to the old school from the Old Rectory, but after that time their journeys into the village took somewhat longer. Mr Boscawen was particularly conscientious in this matter, calling at the school at least twice a week and often more frequently; his wife and daughter also played their part, Mrs and Miss Boscawen superintending the girls' needlework. Indeed in 1881 Mr Nind was ill for two or three weeks and Miss Nellie Boscawen ran the school with one assistant. When her father died on the way to early service on Sunday 8th October 1882, the school was closed for a week as a token of respect; eleven days later, however, the new Rector, Mr Sturkey, and his family were paying their first visit and so the pattern continued. The Rector was usually the person who inspected the registers on behalf of the Managers and signed the Inspector's Report in the log book so that the Managers could act upon its recommendations. A regular annual event was the Diocesan Scripture Examination, conducted in all Church schools, and for a century or more Marchwiel got an encouraging report — sometimes an excellent one. Many former pupils no doubt still possess their certificates — a different colour for each standard.

Attendance was always a prime concern and the master was regularly worried by the weekly percentage of the possible total — 'October 1875: School greatly improved today in numbers — several of the old hands returned for the winter!' In 1876 came a further Education Act which did enforce attendance, so that another regular visitor from now on was the Attendance Officer, who would call at the school for the names of the 'irregulars'. In 1877 Mr Nind wrote 'Several new scholars whose education has been sadly neglected entered this week — no doubt owing to the new Act of Parliament compelling them to attend'. By the following year HM Inspector could write that 'praiseworthy progress has been made ... the writing should be larger and rounder. The specimen needlework was very creditable; rest pretty good or fair'. Again, 'the infants should be talked to in order to improve their intelligence'.

The Inspectors were not always so complimentary about the physical state of the school, often remarking on the dusty cupboards and muddy playground, and above all upon the 'malodorous offices' which graced the rear of the school; these were rebuilt before the First World War but still kept their communal character until complete modernisation took place in the 1950s. Many ex-pupils will remember the 'three-seater' which would arouse such horror in health authorities today.

In the summer of 1883 Mr Nind left and Mrs S W Rogers took over. Immediately children coming late in the morning were detained after school — 'This has brought them more punctual'. Also their fees were increased, as it appeared that Mr Nind had not been charging them enough. Then there were the occasional problems of petty crime and general bad behaviour in the area:

> December 7th 1885: On opening school this morning I find that someone has opened the drawer and taken the Registers away.
>
> December 10th: By today's paper I see that something similar has happened at Isycoed school. There is good ground for supposing both to be part of the riotous proceedings in connection with the Parliamentary election.

Marchwiel had already benefited from the will of Captain Ellis so that money was available for the support of the school, and the Trustees of the Fund applied to be able to use some of this money towards the erection of a master's house on a further portion of glebe land. This was done in 1884, using not more than £250 out of the capital of the Edwards and Ellis Fund. The Log Book notes, during building operations alongside the playground, an occurrence which will surprise no-one: 'Frederick Bradshaw broke his arm while playing on scaffold planks'.

Mrs Rogers left in December 1885 and in 1886 Mr A A Walker was appointed Headmaster. Older residents may remember his two sons Messrs Albert and Percy Walker who were the village postmen in the 1950s and lived with their sister in Stone Cottages near the church. In the next twenty years the timetable was extended, especially in the realm of 'object lessons', on which Her Majesty's Inspectors were particularly keen; models, pictures and a museum cupboard were regularly recommended. Nature study provided a very valuable source in this respect; the infants and lower standards in particular studied birds, insects and small animals and those of us who passed through this class as late as the 1940s will remember with affection the stuffed red squirrel, mounted on its wooden plinth with a nut held securely between its paws, as it had surely been since the turn of the century.

The infants were regularly praised for their progress, but concern was expressed that as the school's numbers increased - from about 70 in 1870 to 90 in the 1890s and later up to 145 — new classrooms needed to be built and in April 1894 Messrs Shone & Son began to erect what was to be the middle section of the school, with another classroom being added in 1899 and opened by Mrs Piercy. At this point the Main Room held 76 children, the classroom next door 31, the new Infants' room 55 and the middle classroom 60. This gave the buildings the appearance which they still possessed when the school closed in 1974.

In 1889 the Trustees of the Edwards and Ellis Fund decided to give prizes for good attendance — £1 for the most regular pupil, 15 shillings for the second and 10 shillings for the third. In addition, to the children who by the report of H M Inspector of Schools showed the greatest proficiency, three prizes of £1, 15 shillings and 10 shillings were awarded. In 1891 elementary education became free, and the achievements of some of the children in Marchwiel began to reflect the rising standards throughout the country. In 1899 the first County Scholarship was awarded to Ernest Cheetham, and in 1901 and 1903 two more members of the same family, Annie and Nellie Cheetham, had the same success. There is, of course, another side to the story; several entries refer to the departure of the best scholars over the years, often to go into domestic service.

With the coming of the twentieth century, national events began to affect school life; the Boer War had not always gone well for Britain, but the relief of Ladysmith in March 1900 was marked by a half holiday, while on May 18th the news of the relief of Mafeking earned a whole day off the following week. Like most others, the school syllabus at this period was very much Empire — orientated in its geography and history lessons; one Inspector had commented in 1880 'The Geography of Standard IV very fair in the colonies, fair in England and pretty fair in Ireland and Scotland. Map knowledge of England and Ireland was pretty fair, of Scotland and

'Top Class', c1905 with Mr A A Walker standing back right. Includes Polly Williams, 4th from the right, front row.   *[Mrs Doreen Jones]*

the colonies moderately fair'. Not once was Wales mentioned; indeed it is not until 1906 that we find the syllabus including Outlines of English History with special reference to the Tudor period and Welsh History, and in class singing, English and Welsh songs. March 1st 1907 seems to have been the first St David's Day marked by a holiday. In 1912 the National Eisteddfod came to Wrexham, and a holiday was granted to enable the children to attend.

The death of Queen Victoria in January 1901 was noted by the Headmaster, and in the following year the school was closed for a total of several weeks to mark the celebration of peace at the end of the Boer War, the coronation of King Edward VII and finally the summer holidays. In September 1902 the newly married Mr and Mrs Yorke of Erddig visited the school; Mr Yorke had already been one of the school Managers for some years and was Treasurer in 1895. In 1903 the new Prince and Princess of Wales (later King George V and Queen Mary) came to Wrexham to be greeted by all the local schoolchildren.

On a more personal note, the Managers' meeting in May 1903 decided that the Headmaster's salary, which had been based on results and average attendance, was no longer reasonable, given the number of recent epidemics; it was therefore fixed at £145 per annum, by unanimous vote. The school had sometimes been closed for two or three weeks at a time by the Wrexham Rural Sanitary Authority, in an attempt to halt the spread of infection, but this did not prevent the sad entry for 1905 which read: 'Three children from one family, who were in school on Friday, were very ill with diphtheria on Saturday, when one case terminated fatally'. There was by now a School Medical Officer, who made regular visits of inspection for the early detection of poor eyesight, lack of cleanliness and, it was hoped, the highly infectious diseases which continued to keep children from the affected district confined at home. We find also that the real threat of tuberculosis was being tackled with lectures to which parents were invited, and also with informative books. It was also presumably for their health that the senior boys took part in a walking competition in October 1903 — held in place of physical exercise, *ie* drill in the playground. The target was five miles, and the first boy to reach it did so in 46 minutes — a nine-minute mile!

Mrs Piercy of Marchwiel Hall continued to play a very active part in school and village life after the death of her husband, and it was thanks to her exertions that £650 had been granted to the school in 1900, and a further £200 later on, by the Trustees of her husband's Trust Fund. In 1906 the Piercy Hall was officially opened and few lessons took place that day, as there was a celebration tea after the ceremony. Three years later in 1909, the new church organ in memory of Mr Piercy was officially opened, and again there was tea in the school to commemorate the occasion.

Another regular event was the Sunday School treat given by the Evans family of The Cottage; for many years a Nonconformist Sunday School had been held in the barn adjoining the main Bangor Road, and it was clearly well attended, despite the small number of chapelgoers in the village. The barn stood until the 1960s, when it was demolished in the cause of road widening at the junction of the Bangor and Overton Roads

By 1907 there were, in addition to the Headmaster, four other teachers, Miss Newill and Miss Carman, both from the village, and two pupil teachers. One of these was Miss Eleanor (Nellie) Cheetham aged 16, who only four years previously had won the open scholarship to Grove Park School. These young people did valuable service in the schools and also prepared for their own future careers. An earlier pupil teacher was Agnes Fisher, who would later be well known in the village as Mrs Samuel, who was postmistress until her retirement in 1946. The Fisher family lived in the cottages opposite the school, and her name appears regularly in the Log Book, winning her first scripture certificate in the Infants' division in 1886 and becoming a pupil teacher in 1895. She later became Headmistress at Worthenbury, but returned temporarily to Marchwiel school in 1915, during the war and after her marriage to Mr Robert Samuel.

In 1908 Mr A G Hunt succeeded Mr Walker, and the average number of pupils by now was in the region of 150, but still it varied quite considerably from week to week. The new Headmaster immediately drew up a syllabus which reflected his very high standards in language teaching, including Parsing and Analysis, English

Standrards 1 & 2, c1921. The teacher on the right is Miss Katie Taylor. Winifred Hunt is seated next to Miss Taylor.   *[Miss Winifred Hunt]*

and Latin prefixes, Greek and Latin roots and chief rules of syntax. By 1913 the Inspector, in giving the school an excellent report in all aspects, commented particularly on the mental arithmetic, in which local shop and market prices were used for calculations. By now there was a small school library, and while the boys worked at their own plots in the school garden, the girls received cookery lessons as well as the established needlework, which had been so carefully supervised since the beginning. In 1912, the boys of Standards IV–VII spent an afternoon at the Rectory, where they received a lesson on Beekeeping from the Rector, assisted by his gardener; three days later, the leaflets issued by the Board of Agriculture and Fisheries dealing with Poultry and Bees (Section 4) were introduced as Readers for the Upper Standards. The Inspector did have reservations, however, about the classical basis of the grammar lessons:

> as the great bulk of the children complete their education in the elementary school, it would perhaps be well to confine the learning of Latin and Greek roots ot a minimum ... It is felt that the time and energy spent on these points could with profit be devoted to the reading and memorising of choice literature and the writing of free composition.

One matter does stand out quite noticeably throughout the whole period of these entries — the teachers were quite often affected by poor health and obliged to miss school; no doubt this was partly due to to their close contact with the diseases incubating among their pupils. In 1910, in the same week as the funeral of King Edward VII, 26 pupils were away with mumps, and not surprisingly, one of the staff also succumbed. More unusually, in the following year, six days after arriving to teach the Infants and Standard I, a young teacher visiting a sick pupil at one of the local farms was bitten by the farmyard dog - her injury led to almost three weeks' absence.

It is well known that the summer of 1914, immediately before the outbreak of war, was oppressively hot, and the Headmaster had to note that several of the Infants were absent suffering from the effects of that heat. The school re-opened after the holiday on the very day that Europe went to war, August 4th, and by September 11th the children were contributing weekly to the Prince of Wales' Fund for the relief of distress 'caused by the Great European War'. A few days later they had collected 16s 4d (82p). The Headmaster did have one male colleague, Mr Kendrick Wynn, until November 1914, but in that month he enlisted in Lord Kitchener's New Army (North Wales Pals' Battalion) and was not immediately replaced, so that 57 children in the top classes had to be taught together. The next few years were difficult ones; supply teachers came and went, a pupil teacher was conscripted for military service, and the boys planted a large plot of waste ground with potatoes to be sold in aid of Red Cross Funds. Despite all the difficulties, however, 1917 was a particularly good year for scholarships and free places, with four being won by Marchwiel pupils — all girls, as it happened. Ethel Cliffe and Bessie Weaver gained Open Scholarships, Marjorie Thelwell a Sub-District Scholarship and Dorothy Allman a free place.

Late in the war food rationing had to be introduced because of enemy attacks on merchant shipping and a general fall in home production. In March 1918, the school was closed for two days so that residents could obtain and complete application forms for butter and meat tickets, which were dealt with by the school staff. Little more is said of the national situation, but in August 1918, when the school re-opened after the summer holidays, we note that several older boys were absent 'being still employed by local farmers', to replace their missing workers..

It is said that the influenza epidemic of 1918 claimed more victims throughout Europe than four years of bitter fighting, and it is ironic that the entry for November 11th makes no mention of the Armistice, only of the fact that the Medical Officer of Health, having closed the school on October 24th because of the outbreak, ordered a further week's closure because of the continued prevalence of illness. There had also been an outbreak of diphtheria earlier in the year, which older residents may well remember. One of the youngest children to suffer this common but often fatal illness lost several of his friends but fortunately recovered to become one of the best known personalities in the village today as well as Mayor of Wrexham in 1983/4 — Councillor J A Davies, formerly of Pontyffrwd.

In Marchwiel, at least, matters had improved by November 18th and the school re-opened to relatively normal conditions. By February 1919 the two male teachers had returned safely from the army and in October of the same year the school was closed for a week to celebrate the Peace Treaty. Bad weather and even such occasions as Wrexham Pleasure Fair could cause early closure fairly frequently, and in 1921 Mr Hunt had to record that there was 'a slight variation in the timetable this morning to oblige a travelling photographer', although this was by no means the first time that the children had faced the camera. In that year also the school garden was inspected by Mr Roberts of Llysfasi, who declared that the spring onions, carrots and parsnips were the best he had seen that year. Only the older boys worked in the garden; the girls aged 12 and over now received lessons in First Aid and the use of a sewing machine as well as minding the baby, at which they were surely already experienced.

1921 was also the first year in which Remembrance Day was observed throughout the country on November 11th itself, with the Silence at 11am precisely, and when for the next thirty years or so the date fell on a school day, a short service was held in the main room, invariably ending with the singing of the hymn 'O God, our help in ages past'. Mr Hunt took great pains to make his pupils aware of their responsibilities, and the teaching they received was reflected in this outstanding report by His Majesty's Inspector in 1921:

> The senior pupils are remarkably alert, have read widely for children of their age and are very well informed ... The work done by Stds VI and VII in Arithmetic, Writing, Reading and Composition deserves unstinted praise and is probably not surpassed by any other school under this Authority. This is done without in the least narrowing the curriculum which includes gardening, a graduated scheme of Hand and Eye training, Drawing in various media etc. Their composition exercises display an unusual command of language, are strikingly free from spelling errors and are written in beautiful handwriting. In arithmetic and algebra the mental work is as quick as the written work is neat and accurate.

Not surprisingly there were two county scholarships in that year, won by Elsie Weaver (whose essay was the best in the county) and Henry Bursey, who later graduated at Lampeter and became curate of Chirk. Children now began to receive book prizes and even writing desks from the Education Authority as rewards for five years' (or more) perfect attendance, and the most regular winners were the

Facing page: Scholarship and Free Place winners, phtographed with Mr Hunt in 1926. Seated (L–R): Winifred Hunt (FP), Edward Clutton (County Scholarship & Top of the County List), Nellie Bursey (FP). Standing (L–R): George Jones (FP), Arthur Weaver (FP).

Weavers of Kiln Farm; Reginald and Emily were joined by Ivy Hughes and Bertram Hunt in 1925, Emily having just come top of the county scholarship list. Over the next few years two more of the family won free places at Grove Park School and running a close second were the Bursey family.

It is not possible to mention all the teaching staff who served Marchwiel School during the period 1874–1974, but one name must find a place; in June 1925 Miss Annie Matthews was appointed to teach the infants in place of Miss Fone, and will be remembered by many in the village today for her discipline and her high standards. She would switch on the lights using her wooden blackboard pointer which, we were told, was a magic wand, and I for one believed her. As Mrs Baker, she left in 1944 to live in the Wirral. 1926 saw another landmark in the school's history. On Good Friday the Headmaster noted the death of the Rector, Archdeacon Fletcher, and by August his successor, Dr (later Canon) E E Thomas was paying his first official visit to the children. He was to become Chairman of the Managers and remained the school's most devoted supporter until his death in 1964.

In June 1926 the Duke of Gloucester had opened the new Wrexham and East Denbighshire War Memorial Hospital and a regular feature over the next few years was the number of fresh eggs collected and donated by the children at regular intervals to the patients; one entry records over a thousand, for which the Matron was suitably grateful. The scholarship examination for that year resulted in Edward Clutton coming top of the whole county, whilst Arthur Weaver, George Jones, Nellie Bursey and Winifred Hunt were awarded free places.

In 1928, Joan Pugh of School Cottages won an open scholarship at the age of 10 and later went on to a university education. She was not the first girl to have done so however; Ellen Linfield had graduated in 1918 having won a sub-district scholarship in 1909. It was at this time that Mr Hunt decided to have a Honours Board erected in the main room to record the first twenty years' successes. It displays the names of all pupils who moved on to secondary education up to 1944 and it remained in position until the school closed in 1974; it is now a feature of the assembly hall in the new building, representing one of the strongest links with the past.

There was, however, a lighter side to school life by now — in 1929 the older pupils were taken on the first long distance school visit, to Port Sunlight and Liverpool Museum, while in the following year they set off for a day at Cadburys' factory in Bournville. Facilities in the school itself, outside lesson time, had not up to that time included much except for blazing fires in the classrooms so that on cold and winter days the children could keep fairly warm and dry (provided that they did not actually fall into the flames, as one unfortunate little girl did at the turn of the century), but in 1932 Horlicks drinks began to be served at dinner time at ½d a cup, and a year or so later school milk was provided at morning break for the same price; we must remember, however, that this was the height of the depression between the

Marchwiel School Staff, 1935. Seated Miss Ethel Mann. Standing (L–R) Miss Annie Matthews, Mr D Emyr Jones, Miss F E Edwards. *[Author]*

Marchwiel School, Standard V, 1936. Included in the photograph are: Mr D Emyr Jones, Doreen Jones, Annie Hughes, Gwen Diggory, Victor Dutton, Dennis While, Ronnie Smith, Doris Lester, Stanley Pritchard, Doris Hall, Edna Morris, Peggy Hughes. [Mrs Edith Jones]

wars, and three parents could not afford the charge. On the other hand, when in September 1934 the whole area was devastated by the news of the Gresford Colliery disaster, in which 267 men were killed, the school was able to raise £4 13s 4½d for the Relief Fund.

In June 1935 Mr Hunt died very suddenly after serving the village for nearly thirty years as Headmaster, organist and choirmaster and also clerk to the council; a supply teacher was sent in to replace him until his successor could be appointed, namely Mr D Emyr Jones, who took up his duties on 1st October of the same year. One of his first tasks was to participate in discussions, involving the Bishop and the Managers, about the possible establishment of a Central Church School based at Marchwiel, the only one in the county, to include the children from Abenbury, Eyton, Isycoed and Erbistock schools, all four of which were experiencing a fall in numbers. It was intended that the Church would finance the buildings and the Local Education Authority the equipment, but the proposal came to nothing.

Football had always been important to the senior boys, and in 1936 a team from the school defeated Tallarn Green boys in the final of the Worthenbury Challenge Cup, for which they were awarded a silver cup. By now the older pupils (up to age 15 until the 1944 Education Act transformed the system) were entering the examinations for the Senior Commercial School which was part of the Denbighshire Technical College — two early successes were those of Alfred Dalby and Doreen Jones. Pupils were now casting their nets more widely; in 1938 Ann Griffiths and Doris Hall won prizes in the *Daily Herald* handwriting competition, while Roger Scott was Highly Commended for an essay as part of Empire Health Week; six years later, aged 19, he was dead, his RAF plane shot down over Hamburg. Several ex-pupils served in the Second World War, of course, but I believe that he was the only one who did not return.

By the time war broke out, there were only eighty pupils in the school, one third of them aged between 11 and 15. Electricity had now been supplied to the village, including the school, and made classes considerably easier, especially in winter. 1939 saw the end of many practices which were not resumed after the war, and one of them was the full attendance prize of a wrist watch. The last two recipients were George and Dilys Pridding, who had not missed a day in five years.

On 1st September the school was closed to prepare for the receipt of blankets and other stores for the use of evacuees, twenty-two of whom were to arrive with their teacher from Liverpool almost as the war began, and were billeted with village families. This was probably the first time, repeated all over Britain, that country met town in such circumstances, and the health of some of the city children caused the authorities such concern that they ordered school to be closed to local pupils until health clearance had been obtained. Much later, in July 1944, more evacuees arrived, this time from Carshalton in Surrey. All pupils were issued with gas masks — red 'Mickey Mouse' models for the younger ones — as the weeks went by, and

rehearsals took place for air raid evacuations. (Marchwiel's wardens were headed by the Rector, with the Headmaster as his deputy.) In September 1940 there was a prolonged night raid which caused classes to be postponed until 10 o'clock the next morning so that children could catch up on their lost sleep; the prize distribution in December of the same year was the one which was interrupted by a daylight raid, when the whole company moved swiftly down to the McAlpine shelter in the school garden and remained there for 45 minutes until the All Clear was sounded. Food rationing was now well established, and in order to ensure that the best use was made of country living, in February 1941 Lady McAlpine and her cook brought a stewpot and helped the older girls to cook vegetables for soupmaking. Two years later the first hot school meals were provided, being delivered from a central kitchen in Hightown at a cost of 5d for the first child in the family, 4d for the second and 3d for the third and any others. Conditions were not ideal, as the heated containers had to be kept until noon and the food served in the main classroom, by which time its taste had deteriorated somewhat, but it was a landmark in its own way. The speaker at that year's prizegiving was Mr Greenwood of Bryn-y-grog, who generously provided the first school radio to enable the children to benefit from schools broadcasting, which was by now developing rapidly. Extension speakers for each classroom were provided by Mr Frank Wellum, one of Wrexham's leading electrical retailers, who had children at the school. Also presented by Mr Greenwood was the silver cup, to be retained for one year by the best scholar.

With the coming of peace in Europe in May 1945, two days' holiday was granted immediately and the evacuees began to return home in due course. The following spring, school had to close because of floods in Bangor and the washing away of several bridges — life was back to normal! At about the same time, the County Music Organiser, Miss Megan Williams, began to interest the school in the making of bamboo pipes, and soon afterwards a pipe band was formed, all of whose members had made their own instruments — and knitted striped covers for them. In 1948 the school was visited by Mr Humphrey Williams, BBC Education Officer for North Wales, who observed the children's reaction to a broadcast lesson on the history of Wales and commented very favourably. In the same year came another landmark — the first school bus.

By 1950 the first Wrexham Trading Estate had replaced the wartime factory, and

Facing page: Marchwiel School, c1957.
Front row (L–R): *Meryl Parry, Pamela Cronin, Edwina Davies,Virginia Birch, Sylvia Griffiths, Joy Hinton, Sheila Williams.* Middle row (L–R): *Gordon Quarmby, Niall Hunt, David Parry, Denis Griffiths, Alan Morris, Colin Martell.* Back row (L–R): *Timothy Reynolds, Kasik Sawin, Freddie Griffiths, Leslie Whalley, Peter Hughes. Mr D Emyr Jones.* *[Author]*

the children of these incoming families began to enrol at the school, so that once again numbers were on the increase. This led to severe overcrowding and it was clear that dining and sanitary facilities were in urgent need of improvement. A new canteen and kitchen were provided in a wooden building which still stands as part of Mr Scott's furniture store, and this brave new world coincided with a one day visit to the Festival of Britain in 1951, when staff, pupils and parents left Wrexham by special train on a journey which they would surely always remember. It was not actually the first of such trips after the war, since a party had visited Windsor and Runnymede in the previous year, and in the 1960s the school ventured abroad for the first time, when a group of older pupils were escorted to Holland.

The school had always marked royal and public occasions in a suitable way, usually with a holiday, as with the marriages of King George V's daughter and sons in the 1920s and 30s, but in 1952 the sudden death of King George VI meant a different kind of commemoration, and all the children from Std III upwards attended a memorial service in church. This was in many ways the end of an era and

Marchwiel School Staff, c1975. Front row (L–R): Mrs Sheila Graver, Mrs Menna Evans, Mr C Bryan Dodd (Headmaster), Mrs Sandra Hughes*, Mrs Pat Hughes*. Back row (L–R): Mrs Jakisch*, Miss Brenda Monk, Miss Leta Smith, Mr J G Owen, Mrs Mary Hunter, Mrs Maureen Lancelotte.   *[C Bryan Dodd]*

Those marked * did not work in the old school.

the beginning of the new age of communication, for the funeral itself was the first state occasion to be seen in this area of North East Wales on television, which had just become possible with the opening of the Sutton Coldfield transmitter. It was followed in eighteen months by the coronation of the present Queen, again watched on the few television sets in Marchwiel at the time, the celebrations ending with a tea at the Piercy Hall, a prize for the best decorated house in the village and a mug for each school child.

Also in the early 1950s, the financial status of the school had changed as its needs increased. It was always a National School linked to the Church but had also been regarded by the county as Non Provided. In 1952 it had received Aided status and two years later it became a Controlled School, receiving full financial support from the Authority. Already, by the Butler Act of 1944, all pupils over the age of eleven were sent to secondary or technical education in Wrexham, but despite the reduction in numbers the state of the school buildings was giving cause for concern, and throughout the 1960s tentative discussions were going on about possible sites for a completely new establishment. Mr D Emyr Jones retired in 1972, just two years before the centenary of the school, and it was his successor, Mr C Bryan Dodd, who presided over the transfer to the Station Road in September 1974. The closure was marked by the presentation of books to each pupil from the Edwards and Ellis Fund, and here the story must end, after a decision which brought the village's history full circle; the new school may not be a church foundation, but appropriately it was christened Ysgol Deiniol — Deiniol County Primary School.

Head teachers since 1841, where recorded.

> 1826 Building
>
> | | |
> |---|---|
> | 1840s | Elias Jones |
> | in office 1851 | Robert Roberts |
> | in office 1861 | Elias Jones |
> | in office 1871 | James Mantle |
>
> 1874 Building
>
> | | |
> |---|---|
> | 1873(?)–83 | James Nind |
> | 1883–85 | Mrs S W Rogers |
> | 1886–1908 | Arthur Aldersea Walker |
> | 1908–35 | Albert G Hunt |
> | 1935–72 | D Emyr Jones |
> | 1972–74 | C Bryan Dodd |
>
> 1874 building closed 1974; new school opened
>
> | | |
> |---|---|
> | 1974–84 | C Bryan Dodd |
> | 1984– | Martin Davies |

8: The Twentieth Century

It seems reasonable to begin an account of Marchwiel's recent history not in 1900 but in 1894, the year when communities throughout the country were empowered to elect a Parish Council with the power to levy a modest penny rate. On December 4th of that year, a parish meeting at the School elected James Carman, gardener, of Bryn-y-grog Lodge, Richard Cliffe, farmer, of Bentleys Farm, John Evans, farmer, of Old Hall, Charles Holland, gentleman, of Bryn-y-grog, George Jones, commercial traveller of the *Red Lion*, William Lee, farmer of Five Fords, Edward Morris, farmer, of The Groves, Thomas Phillips, labourer, of The Fields and Robert Price, leather dresser, of Church Cottages. Ten days later the first meeting took place, and local democracy was on its way. Mr Holland was elected chairman, Mr Evans vice-chairman, and Mr A A Walker of School House was unanimously nominated as clerk, at a salary later fixed at £5 per annum. The vestry books were left in the hands of the Rector, but the Clerk to the Trustees of the charities was requested to hand over all other public books and documents. Early in 1895 the council began to show its determination to improve living conditions in the village, when the clerk was asked to write to the equally new Wrexham Rural District Council about the sanitary condition of village houses and the state of the village pump. We do not know the age of this landmark, but we do know that it stood almost opposite the church, at the end of what was then the garden of the *Red Lion*, and was not removed for many years after the coming of a piped water supply. The enquiry revealed that of 35 cottages inspected, most were in a better condition than had been feared, but the water supply in Sontley was felt to be sadly deficient, especially to the cottages in Bwgan Du Lane (at first spelt 'Burgundy' by the non-Welsh speaking clerk) and it was decided to ask for the well at Stryt-yr-hwch to be analysed. The professional analyst employed by the council to do the work was none other than the local historian A N Palmer, who reported that 'the water is ... dirty, loaded with vegetable organic matter and presenting characteristics which would compel every analyst to condemn it'. He did go on to say, however, that it seemed at source to be good water, and that suitable precautions might make it fit to drink.

At about the same time the council received a letter from the Charity Commissioners regarding their new powers, which were probably causing headaches in parishes all over the country. 'The case of the Marchwiel charities is one of those conundrums which have been provided for us by a humorous legislature. There are three charities ... placed under one scheme: i) Repair of the Parish Church (ecclesiastical) ii) Ellis's (modern) and iii) James ap Edward's (modern).' After 1898 it was possible to separate the first from the other two and appoint Trustees for the latter. Marchwiel's first Edwards and Ellis Trustees were Charles Holland and Richard Cliffe. In the very last month of the century, lists of deserving cases in the parish were drawn up and as a result 42 people received sums varying from £1 to £3, from the Edwards and Ellis Fund; these were distributed just before Christmas 1899 and the practice still continues. £5 was also set aside from the fund for the pupil teacher's salary.

In 1897 came the second local council election, and the new councillors included the Rector Rev E R James, Philip Yorke of Erddig (who was Mayor of Wrexham in the same year) and Edwin Pritchard of Croes-y-mab. This was the year of Queen Victoria's Diamond Jubilee, and numerous ideas for celebrations were put forward, including a tea for children and supper for adults, a reading room, the drainage of the school yard, a fountain, endowed beds in Wrexham Infirmary, a parish hall, and the possibility of gas in the village so that street lighting could be installed. Electric street lamps were eventually erected in the 1950s!

By 1895 the new Wrexham to Ellesmere railway had been built, and the council was concerned that the traditional footpath was being obliterated in parts of the new Station Road. Walkers crossing the line were sometimes at risk, and in 1899 the Wrexham and Ellesmere Railway Company was asked to provide either a footbridge or a tunnel at the station at a spot crossed by the old footpath, but nothing came of this. It was also reported that the lamp erected in the Station Road was overshadowed by bushes, so that the walk was quite dangerous in darkness. Furthermore, graves in the churchyard were being flooded by damaged water pipes in the road, and the railway company agreed to repair them.

With the death of the old Queen in 1901 and the coronation of King Edward VII in the following year, further problems faced this very conscientious council, such as how best to celebrate the occasion. There were three main suggestions — a good water supply for Sontley and Stryt-yr-hwch, provision of reading room facilities in the new infants' classroom at the school, and a monument and lamp on the site of the old pump. The last was rejected, but before very long the piped water supply was extended from Marchwiel Hall to Sontley and also from the Rectory to Cock Bank.

Clearly the village had every confidence in its elected representatives and left them to get on with the job, if the low attendance at the annual parish meeting is any guide. In 1906 only two councillors and the clerk attended, so no business could be transacted. In regular council meetings, however, failure to attend reasonably regularly was eventually followed by disqualification. Overseers of the poor were still being elected and when Mr Cain Ratcliffe, the landlord of the *Red Lion* (retired coachman at Erddig) took office in 1908, he asked for an assistant as the work was still onerous, especially the drawing up of valuation lists to calculate the Poor Rate. (Mr Ratcliffe was in any case a busy man, as the special excursion stage coaches still stopped occasionally on the cobbled frontage of the *Red Lion*). Most of Marchwiel's poor at this time were mostly the elderly; it is on record that there was no unemployment whatsoever in the parish and the farmers were regularly shorthanded at harvest time.

We also note the beginning of modern traffic hazards at this period — it was reported in 1909 that there were dangerous bends near both Top House and Holly Hedge, on the Bangor Road, and the owners were asked if they would agree to sell land to the County Council for widening schemes. Soon afterwards the main roads were tarred for the first time, in order to keep the dust down. In 1913 the centre of the village took on much of its modern appearance with the building of the Post Office and adjoining house. There was much enthusiasm for a telephone call office also, but this was delayed for the time being.

There already existed in the village the Marchwiel Working Men's Guild, established through the generous bequest of Mr Piercy of Marchwiel Hall 'for the purposes of promoting the social and intellectual welfare of and providing reasonable recreation for the men and youths of the village of Marchwiel'. In 1906 it was decided to extend this provision with a building which has served the village ever since — the Piercy Hall. Trustees were appointed, including Mr Evans of Old Hall, Mr Sam: Clutton, of Stone House, brickmaker, Mr Arthur Pashley, brickmaker, Mr Charles Samuel of Pontyffrwd, farmer, and Mr Benjamin Piercy of Gerwyn, son of the benefactor. A constitution was drawn up declaring that the Hall

> shall be primarily available for the purposes of the said Guild, provided that the same shall ... be appropriated as a reading or recreation room for the use of all men and youths of the age of sixteen years or upwards, resident in the village of Marchwiel or within a distance of three miles therefrom, who in the opinion of the Committee shall belong to the artisan or labouring classes and shall be sober and industrious and of good character, but without regard to their political or religious opinions.

The last condition was the personal wish of Mrs Sarah Piercy and the solid redbrick building stands as a tribute to her husband's generosity and the hard work of those who formulated the rules ninety years ago.

The Liberal government which had been re-elected in 1910 was keen to impose a tax on land values, and a conference was called in 1913 to which Marchwiel was invited to send representatives. The agricultural interests on the Parish Council prevailed, however, and the invitation was refused on the grounds that land was overtaxed already. By the following year, of course, Europe was at war and the farmers were asked to ensure that the maximum amount of cereal crop was produced, since imported grain could not be relied upon in the face of naval warfare, and of course they all responded positively. A War Distress Fund was set up, as well as the Prince of Wales' Relief Fund, and a committee nominated to organise collections in the village. Members were Mrs J J Hughes, Top House, Mrs Ernest Hughes, Old Sontley, Miss Roberts, Stryt-yr-hwch, Miss Penry, Bryn Afon, Mrs Lloyd Jones, Grove Terrace and Mr J W Evans, The Cottage. Parliament was also encouraging recruitment, but the Council felt that as many young men had already enlisted voluntarily and that there was also a Civic Guard and Rifle Club, more effort was not required. Later, however, it was obliged to take a census of all men of military age and submit the list to the East Denbighshire Committee. In common with the rest of the country the village was to suffer sad losses by 1918, and the names of those who died can be seen on a brass plaque behind the pulpit in the church; three of the four who died, Thomas Jones, Herbert Ankers and Thomas Lloyd, were privates in the Royal Welsh Fusiliers (the spelling was changed to 'Welch' in 1920), while the fourth, Thomas Hughes, also a private, had enlisted in the Shropshire Light Infantry. They are also now commemorated (November 1997) by a modern sculpture in the Peace Garden which has been created at the Piercy Hall end of the new cemetery.

The rest of Marchwiel's war effort was concentrated on self-sufficiency, with a request to Mrs Ratcliffe of the *Red Lion* to allow the adjoining field to be used as allotments, while seed potatoes were distributed for both allotments and gardens.

Mr Walker had been succeeded as headmaster in 1908 by Mr A G Hunt, and on the death of the previous clerk in 1916 Mr Hunt was appointed at a salary of £30 per year. This was to be a busy time for him; in 1917 came the death of the chairman, Mr J W Evans, Old Hall, who had left to the parish his land next to the churchyard so that a new burial ground could be opened. It was also agreed that after the Disestablishment of the Church in Wales, (passed by Parliament in 1914 but postponed until 1920, after the end of the war) the Parish Council would be responsible for the new cemetery, but it was not actually opened until 1935.

Soon after the end of the war a curious letter was sent to all parishes from the District Council, offering to any interested authority the opportunity to keep items of captured German military hardware. Many had refused the offer and some of Marchwiel's councillors felt the same, but the Rector, Canon Fletcher, made an impassioned speech about the virtue of patriotism and pointed out that Marchwiel's Volunteer Corps had been one of the first in the country. No further mention is made of the unwanted gift, however.

Peace was celebrated in the village with a firework display organised by the Denbighshire Beacon and Bonfire Committee. The name of Mr Fowles, gardener at Marchwiel Hall, had been submitted to the County Council as he was a responsible and reliable person 'with some experience in the letting off of fireworks', and no doubt an exhilarating evening was enjoyed. On a more serious note, the first ever Poppy Day Appeal in the village raised £7.

Still in 1919, the Council was asked to support a resolution to establish Wrexham

Canon William Henry Fletcher,
Rector of Marchwiel, 1907–26.
[Miss Winifred Hunt]

as the administrative centre for North Wales 'in any scheme of self-government which might be set up in the future' and did so, little guessing, one imagines, how distant that date was. (The referendum of 1997 was held as this chapter was being written.) In November 1919, however, a special parish meeting voted against a plan to include Marchwiel within an enlarged Wrexham Borough, although nearly eighty years later this is exactly what has happened. This was the year for a new council to be elected, and the nine names were: Archdeacon Fletcher and Messrs Horace Evans (Old Hall), J J Hughes (Top House), Wm. Huxley (High Leigh), Job Jones (Marsh Farm), E Lloyd Jones (Grove Terrace), J H Latham (Bryn Moyle), Thos. Morris (Clay Farm) and Charles Morris (The Groves).

The main peacetime problem throughout the country was the provision of adequate housing, and in Marchwiel six cottages had been condemned or already demolished, with three others condemned before 1914 still temporarily occupied.

There was now an urgent need for homes for farm workers and returning servicemen, and the council also discussed the possibility of a new colliery being opened on Mr Yorke's land, although this did not materialise. The District Council was asked to build at least 25 houses, and these were later put up along the Bangor Road, although not until 1933.

A sale catalogue earlier in the century for Croes-y-mab Farm mentioned that 'motor buses pass the door regularly throughout the day', and although this phrase would have surprised those who depended upon them during the Second World War and the 1950s, it is true that the service was greatly appreciated, especially the personal touch provided by the family firm of Williams and Hodson, who operated from Providence House. For many years their buses were chartered to take children and adults of the Sunday School and church on their annual outing, which was usually to Rhyl, leaving the village virtually deserted for the day. In 1932 the fare from Bryn-y-grog to Wrexham went up from 2d to 3d and that from Overton up to 8d from 7d single, with the return fare being abolished, to great public indignation. By 1936 all buses from the area were using the Beast Market as a terminus, an the clerk's duties included the request for bus shelters, which again did not materialise for many a long year. Traffic through the village was increasing at quite a rate, and the position of the school on such a busy road was the cause of some concern; the Rector, as chairman of the school managers, felt obliged to write to the Council suggesting a Belisha Beacon opposite the school gate to minimise the danger, but no action was taken for many years, despite the clerk's letters.

In 1935 King George V and Queen Mary celebrated their Silver Jubilee and in the same year the parish meeting was the first to be attended by ladies. Mrs Bellis, Mrs T Williams and Mrs G Jones were asked for their views on the best form of celebrating the Jubilee, which doubtless included the provision of countless cakes and cups of tea at some stage of the proceedings. The King died early the following year, so that by 1937, despite the abdication of King Edward VIII, the country was preparing for another coronation, when George VI succeeded his brother and retained the date in May which had originally been planned for Edward. Marchwiel celebrated with tea in the Piercy Hall for all children and over 60s. Just over a year later, in July 1938, the clerk received an ominous warning of things to come — arrangements for ARP (Air Raid Precautions) lectures to be held throughout the district. Reference has already been made to the underground air raid shelter in the school garden — there was also a conventional brick shelter convenient to the Bangor Road houses; other precautions included the protection of the classroom windows of the school, those at the top of the playground, by a brick wall which mercifully was never put to its intended use but served as an invaluable ally in games of hide and seek. The school in fact became the ARP post, with the Rector as Head Warden and the Headmaster as his deputy. The latter, Mr D Emyr Jones, appointed in 1935 to succeed Mr Hunt, had been elected to the Council in 1937 but

resigned in 1940 on being appointed its clerk - an office he was to hold for over forty years.

It was the Parish Council which was called upon to co-ordinate the various fundraising efforts which went on throughout the next six years — 'Lend to Win' in 1940 and 'Warship Week' in 1941 for example. Newspapers and scrap iron were collected for salvage, and the farming councillors agreed to supply the necessary sacks. As the war went on, one new feature of village life was the presence of German and Italian prisoners of war on several of the farms; one or two in fact stayed in the area for a time after 1945 when peace came. It would not be true to suggest that Marchwiel was unaffected by the possibility of air attack, because it was not much over a mile from the large Royal Ordnance Factory which was built on a 1,400 acre site bordering the parish, with Five Fords, Pumrhyd and Tyddyn Daniel to its South East and Hugmore Lane and Redwither Lane to the West. Building was approved in July 1939 and it was in full production by February 1941, at a cost of £10.9 million. Ten thousand workers travelled daily to and from it, producing cordite for the munitions industry, and by no means all were local; they were recruited from all over the country and had lodgings throughout the area. The bus stands which coped with the traffic remained for a good many years after the war, and the site has now become the Wrexham Industrial Estate.

In one respect Marchwiel had a unique part to play in a little- publicised aspect of the conflict with Nazi Germany; the Rector, Dr Thomas, was a distinguished German scholar and philosopher with degrees from the universities of Jena and Heidelburg and was employed by the authorities to hold lectures and discussions with German prisoners in the cause of 'denazification'. Some years later he gave an interview in which he spoke of the courteous reception which he received from many of the prisoners, who listened carefully to what he had to say, although from the more hardbitten submarine crews and SS men he had a less pleasant reaction. I like to think that some of his predecessors, like the kindly Maurice Anwyl, the scholarly Humphrey Ffoulkes and Samuel Strong, and the public-spirited Montagu Luxmoore, would approve of his efforts. In addition to his interest in German philosophy, he wrote a novel about life in rural Wales, called *Where Eagles Fly, No Bird Sings*.

In August 1945, with the coming of peace with Japan and the ceasing of all hostilities, the Ministry of Health sanctioned the spending of money for victory celebrations, and a sports afternoon was held on the field next to Smithy Cottages (now Berwyn Close), followed by tea for the children and a social in the evening. Some will remember the treasure hunt on the field, when at least one ten-shilling

Facing page: Rev Dr Evan Edward Thomas and members of the Marchwiel Mothers' Union, Southport, c1930. Mr Sam Williams, driver of the Williams & Hodson coach is standing on the step.

note was concealed under a (dry) cowpat for the more enterprising to win. A week later, on August 23rd, there was a social for the over 60s, the total sum officially allowed being £3, although of course there were many generous donations.

Several of the village's young men had of course been absent on active service and the lives of their families did not return to normal until they were all demobilised by 1946. A 'Welcome Home Fund' was set up by the council, and in due course the returning servicemen were each presented with a leather wallet. As if to celebrate the return to complete normality, the County Council agreed to to pay one shilling per child and 1s 3d for each person over 65 for another victory tea, followed by a film show in the school. It should be explained that this was a series of silent films, one a Charlie Chaplin and another of the 1934 wedding of the Duke of Kent to Princess Marina of Greece — but in those relieved and uncomplicated days they were received with much pleasure.

During the war local councils had been given authority to request the ploughing up of footpaths in the cause of extra food production, but in 1946 this was withdrawn and paths and stiles were to be repaired and restored to their pre-war state. As had happened nearly thirty years earlier, there was now an acute housing shortage as the returning forces and those already employed on the new Trading Estate needed homes. (Strangely, however, the actual population of the village by 1951 was only 626, the same figure as 1901, after a rise to 695 in 1921.) Piercy Avenue was built in the early 1950s and from then on development was steady. By 1955, after a very long wait, street lighting was installed and a year later a 30 mile limit was imposed from Croes-y-mab through the village, signifying the rapid increase in road traffic after the war. The Cheshire View estate was begun in 1963, while in the late sixties Top House Farm was completely demolished and the land sold to become, from 1972 onwards, part of the Ridgeway and Deiniol Avenue.

This brings us back to the story of the railway. A seemingly permanent feature of village life throughout the period, at least for those living close to the church and Bangor Road, was the station, whose approach road had caused such concern to the first parish councillors. The Wrexham–Ellesmere Railway, the construction of which had devastated so much of the town of Wrexham, provided a reliable and comfortable service for those who could manage the walk down to the station, secure in the knowledge that even if the train were to be late, there was a warm waiting room to accommodate them. Local farmers used the railway to transport their milk, and the weighbridge indicated a flourishing goods traffic. There were not many trains in a day, but the 8.30am service took children to the Wrexham secondary schools, as well as office workers into the town. Perhaps its most attractive feature was that the train entered the station facing would-be passengers as they raced down the Station Road, and would never leave without the latecomers — at least the ones the driver could spot in time. All this came to an end in the Beeching era, and in 1962, after several years of uncertainty about its future, the last train left Wrexham Central Station at its usual time of 9pm, calling at Hightown on its journey to Marchwiel, then on to Ellesmere via Sesswick and Bangor. One of the passengers was Alderman Herbert Hampson, who remembered his journey on the first train in 1895, when the return fare from Marchwiel to Wrexham was 2d. The station buildings survived for a number of years as the premises of a small business firm, but this phase also came to an end and the whole site was eventually cleared, including the track. It is currently being developed for housing.

It is possible to argue that since the 1960s the village has become almost a suburb of Wrexham as the town has expanded; with the building of the new stretch of road, the northern boundary of the parish at Kings Mills Bridge is no longer on the main highway, although the southern end at Cock Bank, Cross Lanes and Sontley has not changed nearly so much. New building has brought in a greatly increased population, which at the last census (1991) stood at over 1,400 — more than doubled in forty years. The Smithy (opposite the former school), which was used until just before the Second World War for its original purpose, has now been demolished, and the village no longer has its own police officer; reorganisation of policing has meant the sale of the police station, built in the 1930s, although there was certainly an officer in the village at the turn of the century, when one of the Forest View houses was used as the police station. Very few residents are now employed in agriculture, in marked contrast to previous generations, most now travelling either to the Trading Estate or Wrexham or to Dairy Crest which occupies the former site of Cadburys' chocolate factory. At the same time, however, several of the farms in the area have remained in the same family for generations. The village continues to be, as we hope that it always will be, a closeknit community enjoying the beautiful countryside on its doorstep without having to suffer the real hardships with which earlier inhabitants had to struggle.

Bibliography

Printed Sources

Archaeologia Cambrensis Various articles published between 1868 and 1890
Byegones	Articles 1886, 1888
Corbet, A E	*The Family of Corbet and its Life and Times* (1915)
Cymmrodorion Society	*Y Bywgraffiadur Cymreig (The Dictionary of Welsh Biography)*
Dodd, A H	*History of Wrexham* (1957)
	Welsh & English in East Denbighshire (1940)
	Studies in Stuart Wales (1971)
Ellis, T P	*The First Extent of Bromfield & Yale* (1924)
Garnett, Oliver	*Erddig* (1995)

Griffiths, Eric   *Philip Yorke I, Squire of Erthig* (1995)
Inventory of Ancient Monuments in Wales — Denbighshire (1911)
Jones-Mortimer, H M C   *High Sheriffs of Denbighshire 1541–1970* (1971)
Lloyd, J Y W   *History of Powys Fadog* Vols II & III (1881)
Lhuyd, Edward   *Parochialia* (1699—ed Rupert Morris, 1909-11)
Myddelton, W M   *Chirk Castle Accounts 1606–1666* (1908)
Palmer, A N   'The Broughtons' article in *History of Holt, Isycoed*
                             and Bangor Isycoed (1991)
Report on the State of Education in Wales 1847 Vol 3
Thomas, D R   *History of the Diocese of St Asaph* (1910)
Tucker, Norman   *Denbighshire Officers in the Civil War*
                             The Civil War in North Wales
Calendar of Returns Relating to Wales – Religious Census 1851 (1981)
Wrexham Advertiser various issues 1956
Wrexham Leader various issues 1970s and 1980s

Manuscript Sources

Denbighshire Record Office
                        Census Returns 1851-91
                        Deeds, various
                        Glebe Terriers 1791 and 1856
                        Poor Law – Overseers' Accounts 1677–1771
                        Parish Council Minutes (3 Vols 1894–1958)
                        Parochial Church Council Minutes (1920–37)
                        Transcripts and microfilm of Parish Registers
                        Tithe Accounts and Maps 1841
                        Vestry Books i) Ecclesiastical 17th and 18th centuries
                                     ii) Civil 1800–64
                        Wynnstay Papers
Flintshire Record Office
                        Erddig Papers
                        Galltfaenan Papers
                        Gwysaney Papers
                        Kenyon and Plas Power Estate Papers
National Library of Wales
                        Chirk Castle Papers (Vol II)
                        Carreglwyd Papers
                        St Asaph Diocesan Records (Visitations of 1738, 1790,
                        1799, 1809)
Shropshire Records Centre
                        Shropshire Genealogies Vol 3 (George Morris, 1838)